FOREWORD BY
PHYLLIS SCHLAFLY

FedEd

The New Federal
Curriculum and
How It's Enforced

ALLEN QUIST

**MAPLE RIVER
EDUCATION COALITION**
St. Paul, Minnesota

Fed Ed: The New Federal Curriculum and How It's Enforced
Copyright ©2002 Allen Quist
All rights reserved

Cover Design by Alpha Advertising
Interior design by Pine Hill Graphics

Published by the Maple River Education Coalition
1402 Concordia Avenue
St. Paul, MN 55104
651-646-0646
www.EdWatch.org
mredco@mcleodusa.net

ISBN: 0-9675196-1-6

Printed in the United States of America.

Foreword

The United States of America was conceived in liberty. Our nation was founded on the recognition that all people are created equal and are endowed by their Creator with certain unalienable rights, including the rights to life, liberty and the pursuit of happiness. Founded on these principles, our nation is a model of freedom for the rest of the world.

National sovereignty is essential to our nation's freedom. Indeed, national sovereignty is the first principle cited in our Declaration of Independence:

> When in the Course of human Events, it becomes necessary for one People to dissolve the Political Bands which have connected them with another, and to assume among the Powers of the Earth, the separate and equal Station to which the Laws of Nature and of Nature's God entitle them....

Our nation's schools are fundamental to the preservation of our freedom. Whether these schools are public, private, or home schools, these institutions of learning have always been free to pursue truth, knowledge and virtue as they have seen fit. Our schools taught American history and government so that our children would learn about our free system of government along with the fundamental principles that are responsible for our freedom. History is all about ideas, and America was founded on, and has always taught its children, the ideas behind our being a free nation of free people.

Freedom, however, has a price. Eternal vigilance is part of that price, and America must be vigilant today even as America has been vigilant in the past. We always have and always will face serious threats to our freedom. Some of these threats come from forces outside our country. Some of the threats come from within. Some of the threats come from without and from within at the same time.

This book, *Fed Ed: The New Federal Curriculum And How It's Enforced*, describes one of these threats to our freedom. Most Americans know little about this threat, even though many Americans are sensing that something is very much amiss with our system of education.

American citizens are puzzled, for example, about their children being forced to choose careers by the eighth grade or even sooner. They wonder why schools increasingly devote their time and attention to meeting federal requirements even though, under the Tenth Amendment to the U.S. Constitution, education is a state and local prerogative. Parents are concerned about the new emphasis on "process" as opposed to knowledge. Parents are troubled by the dramatic decline in scores on academic tests, such as the recent 80-point decline in the SAT. At the same time, colleges and businesses wonder how they can effectively cope with students and workers who cannot read well enough to succeed in high school, let alone graduate.

As the reader will discover in this book, all these trends are interrelated. These trends are indicators of more fundamental concerns— questions about the very purpose of education in our country; issues about who should decide what is taught in our schools; and, most significant of all, the realization that the federal government is increasingly running our schools and is doing so in a manner that is inconsistent with our being a free country.

This book is one of the important works of our time. It is full of information that is carefully documented and available for everyone. Most important, the book is dedicated to keeping our nation and our people free.

Phyllis Schlafly

Acknowledgments

A number of people have contributed significantly to the research and writing of this book. They include past President of the Maple River Education Coalition, Renee Doyle; researcher and speaker on the new education system, Michael Chapman; popular speaker and State Senator, Michele Bachmann; writer and speaker, Dr. Karen Effrem; and Vice-President of the Maple River Education Coalition, my wife, Julie Quist.

In particular, I would like to thank Barbara Mattson who did the proofreading and editing; Dr. Karen Effrem who contributed most of the research for Chapter 16 ("Taking Over Baby Education"); and Julie Quist who contributed much of the research and most of the encouragement for the entire book.

Allen Quist

Contents

PART IV
The Road Back

APPENDICES

PART I

The Nature of the
New Federal Curriculum

CHAPTER ONE

Restructuring America

Many citizens are beginning to notice the profound changes taking place in America's system of education. What are these changes all about? Stated simply, the restructuring of American education is all about restructuring America. The new education system intends to transform America from what it is today into something far different. Backers of the new system say that radical changes must be made in order to "prepare our children and the rest of society for the future." Profound changes must also be made, they say, in America's system of government.

Shirley McCune, a well-known speaker and writer on the new education system, has made the case for these changes in her article, "Restructuring Education." Why is American education being transformed? McCune said the reason is as follows:

> Our society has undergone **profound economic, demographic, and social transformation**—a transformation that impacts virtually every aspect of our **individual and**

collective lives. It is the manifestation of a **new era of civilization**...and the movement from a **national to a global society.** Virtually every institution is forced to restructure to meet a changed environment and changed needs. [Emphasis added, *http://www.net/-building/crfut_mccune.html.*]

This statement by McCune is an accurate summary of the thinking behind the new education system (including the new Federal Curriculum). This thinking, as McCune says, welcomes a "social transformation" that helps bring in a "new era of civilization" which culminates in "the movement from a national to a global society."

Notice the tense of the verbs McCune used in her description. She began with the past perfect tense and quickly moved to the present tense. McCune is not speaking of some past or future transformation of our society; she is describing what has been happening and is happening right now.

Much of what she says involves government policy. It involves education policy in particular, but other government policy as well. The changes additionally require new government policies that will play a key role in ushering in the transformation of American society.

The news media, however, has reported little about these important changes (see Chapter 5). Major policy decisions require public debate, but how can the public debate the changes when it doesn't know they are taking place?

Major government policy changes also require legislative debate. For the most part, however, that legislative debate has not occurred. Why not? As is true with citizens generally, most legislators, too, are unaware of the huge policy changes being made. The reason is this: Most legislators would oppose these policy changes if they knew what they were and if they knew how they were being put into place. The minority of legislators who do understand the new system, are, for the most part, its advocates.

The transformation of American society is taking place on many fronts. Its one primary focal point is the restructuring of education. At the same time, restructuring education is not the ultimate goal, but it is the means to that goal. The ultimate goal is the restructuring of government, a goal that is now well underway. If the transformation of

American (and world) government is completed, the transformation of all of society can then be expected to follow.

The critical link in this chain of events is the restructuring of education. The restructuring of education, in turn, focuses on restructuring the curriculum. That is, the restructuring of education focuses on the question of what our children are being taught in the schools. How is this school curriculum being determined? By parents? No. By elected school boards? No. By teachers and administrators? Not any more. By state legislators? Not to any significant degree. The school curriculum is now being dictated by the federal government.

Who are the visionary change-agents behind the restructuring of America? There are many. A list of possible/likely candidates should include:

+ Former President and former First Lady Bill and Hillary Clinton.
+ Marc Tucker, Director of the National Center for Education and the Economy NCEE).
+ Lauren Resnick, Co-director of the New Standards Project.
+ Charles Quigley, Director of the Center for Civic Education (CCE).
+ Margaret Stimmon Branson, Associate Director of the CCE.

The federal government, at this time, is determining the curriculum in the schools by means of the new Federal Curriculum. The purpose of this book is to provide a description of how the federal government took over education policy-making in our country including taking over the school curriculum. It will also describe and document both the characteristics and the contents of the new Federal Curriculum. Finally, the book will describe how the entire system is now being implemented.

Major policy decisions require citizen and legislative debate. This book is dedicated to equipping America's citizens and legislators with the information necessary for that debate. This book is written in the hope that the needed debate can begin.

CHAPTER TWO

Taking Control of the Curriculum

In days gone by, the curriculum in our schools was stated as subject areas, also known as "academic disciplines." The curriculum was organized around subjects like math, reading, history, and science. Not any more. Shirley McCune, in her article, correctly said:

> The curriculum may be organized in any number of ways—around themes (magnets), special interests, alternative programs, or work in the community. It must develop **interdisciplinary** relationships and **culminate in action or application** activities if it is to be relevant to future needs. [Emphasis added.]

Notice, as stated by McCune, that the new curriculum is not organized around academic subjects. Those subjects are still there in a superficial way, but they don't make up the real curriculum. As McCune said, the real curriculum consists of "themes" that are "interdisciplinary" and that "culminate in action or application" that is "relevant to future needs." This book will describe the new Federal Curriculum as themes, not as academic subjects, because, as McCune is correct in saying, themes are what the new curriculum is really all about.

As McCune pointed out, these curriculum themes are interdisciplinary, and they involve action of some kind. As shall be demonstrated in subsequent chapters, the action portion of the themes normally involves political action. This political action, in turn, requires restructuring our system of government in significant ways. As a consequence, America now has a highly politicized system of education. It is politicized in two ways: (1) The new Federal Curriculum is a product of political actions—new laws and regulations that have dramatically altered our education system; and (2) the curriculum themes themselves are directed toward additional restructuring of America's system of government.

How did the federal government manage to take control of the nation's curriculum? It did so by means of three bills passed by Congress in 1994 and signed into law by then President Bill Clinton. These three bills were: (1) the Goals 2000: Educate America Act (commonly known as "Goals 2000"), (2) the School-to-Work: Opportunities Act (abbreviated as "School-to-Work" or "STW"), and (3) the funding (appropriations) bill for most federal education programs (known as HR6).

The overall effect of these interconnected bills was that state and local governments could no longer determine education policy. The federal government would now be in charge of all education policy in the United Stated, including the curriculum—even though the Tenth Amendment to the U.S. Constitution stipulates that education is reserved for state and local governments.

Specifically, HR6 said:

> (1)(A) The Secretary [of Education] is **authorized to carry out a program** to enhance the third and sixth National Education Goals [of Goals 2000] **by educating students** about the history and principles of the United States, including the Bill of Rights, and to foster civic competence and responsibility. [Emphasis added, Title X, Section 10601 a.]

Translated this means that the federal government will now "carry out a program" by "educating students" on what is meant by "the history and principles of the United States." The federal government would now also determine what the "Bill of Rights" really means and what information and attitudes students must learn under the heading of "civic competence and responsibility."

How would the official federal government knowledge and values be determined? HR6 answered that question when it said:

> (B) Such programs shall be known as "We the People: The Citizen and the Constitution." (2) The **programs shall (A) continue and expand the educational activities of the "We the People: The Citizen and the Constitution"** program **administered by the Center for Civic Education;** and (B) enhance student attainment of challenging content standards in civics and government. [Emphasis added, Title X, Section 10601 a.]

It is difficult to overstate the significance of this law. The law states that one nongovernmental organization (NGO) known as the "Center for Civic Education" had been designated by federal law to write the federal education standards for civics and government. That is: **This one organization, the Center for Civic Education (CCE) will determine, by force of federal law, what must be taught in all our nation's schools regarding civics and government.** This single organization would dictate what was true and what was important in these academic areas. There would be no review of its dictates by Congress. There would be no review of its dictates by American citizens. Our schools would have nothing to say about what this one group determined was true and important regarding civics and government. One organization (NGO) would determine the new National Curriculum in these areas, and no one else would have anything to say about it.

It is amazing that such a law could pass in a free country. Where was the public debate? What happened to the Tenth Amendment to the Constitution? How could such a law pass the Congress? The reason it could pass is that most of the senators and representatives never read the fine print in this bill (and most other bills that often number over a thousand pages). Senators and representatives rely on their staff and the Congressional leadership to tell them what is in the bills. Apparently the staff didn't realize the significance of the wording quoted above (not unusual), and apparently those in leadership who knew what the bill meant didn't tell the other senators and representatives what was happening (also, not unusual).

This is the kind of law that most senators and representatives know "...doesn't pass the smell test." To this day, however, most senators and representatives have no idea that they passed the above wording into law. Most legislators would have voted against the bill if they had known what it said and what it meant. The architects of the new education system know, of course, that their success depends on most legislators being ignorant of what is in the bills.

Who is going to pay for the enactment of this Federal Curriculum? That matter was also settled by HR6. The law said:

> (3) The Secretary [of Education] is authorized to award a grant or enter into a contract with the Center for Civic Education to carry out the program described in paragraph (1). [Emphasis added, Title X, Section 1061 a.]

Once again, the law says that this one NGO—the Center for Civic Education—was authorized to write the National Curriculum in civics and government. The citizens were then required to pay whatever expenses this organization incurred. Absolutely incredible. The Department of Education was not required to allow bids or to consider any other groups for writing the national standards. The CCE had an exclusive inside track.

It should also be recognized that NGOs, such as the Center for Civic Education, never face the voters in any election. If the citizens of American don't like what the Center for Civic Education has done, they have little opportunity to object. CCE officers needn't run for public office. Like all other NGO members, they answer only to the NGO itself.

To make matters worse, in December of 2002, in passing the "No Child Left Behind" education bill, Congress reenacted similar language which authorizes and funds the Center for Civic Education to continue its control of the Federal Curriculum. Freedom in our land is very much in jeopardy, and most members of Congress have no idea about what is happening.

As the law authorized, the Center for Civic Education has since determined what the federal government's standards (Federal Curriculum) for civics and government now are. The standards were published in 1994—the same year the CCE was authorized to create them. (The standards were obviously ready to go before the law was passed.)

This book of standards can be purchased from:

Center for Civic Education
5146 Douglas Fir Road
Calabasas, CA 91302-1467
Toll Free (800) 350-4223
Fax (818) 591-9330

The price is $12.00 each plus 10% for postage and handling. The publisher says:

These standards specify what students should know and be able to do in the field of civics and government. Grades K-12. 1994. 187 pages. ISBN 0-89818-155-0.

It is time that America's citizens and elected officials know the truth about the takeover of the curriculum of our nation's schools by this one organization, the Center for Civic Education (CCE). This takeover amounts to a bloodless coup. The content of our nation's schools, which should be and in the past was determined by the citizens and elected leaders of our nations, is now controlled by one small group of individuals. Are we, the citizens of the United States, going to sit back and allow this to continue?

We now turn to the question: *What are the overall characteristics of this new Federal Curriculum?*

CHAPTER THREE

Rewriting the
Nation's Curriculum

A s has been pointed out, the new Federal Curriculum is a politicized curriculum. Every curriculum theme in the new system of education involves political action and/or governmental restructuring. The civics and government curriculum forms the core curriculum of the entire new Federal Curriculum.

For that reason, it should not surprise us that the *National Standards for Civics and Government* makes the following statement:

> Civic education instead should be considered central to the purposes of American education. [Emphasis added, p. 2 of the standards.]

That is, the new national standards themselves clarify that the civics and government standards form the heart and center of the new Federal Curriculum. The civics and government curriculum is the core curriculum. Since the 1994 law, HR6, gave the Center for Civics Education (CCE) the authority to determine the national standards in civics and government, the standards written by the CCE addition-ally have the effect of law. This means that by force of federal law the CCE's standards for civics and government are now the primary and central feature of the new Federal Curriculum. The CCE's standards form the core curriculum for our nation's schools.

The *National Standards for Civics and Government* also says:

> **Achievement of these standards should be fostered** not only by explicit attention to the civic education in the cur-riculum, but **also in** related subjects such as **history, liter-ature, geography, economics, and the sciences** and by the informal curriculum of the school, the pattern of relations maintained in the school and its governance. [Emphasis added, pp. V, VI.]

As stated above, schools are now required to teach the national standards for civics and government in most, if not all, other subjects. The entire curriculum in each school must be redone to integrate the new National Curriculum in civics and government into the various classes taught throughout the school day.

How does this integration of civics and government into other subjects take place? One example was printed in the Minneapolis *StarTribune* newspaper on April 9, 2000, in an article called "Integrated Math." This article included a photograph of a local math class where all the students, and the teacher, were squeezed into a far corner of a classroom. The caption under the photo explained the lesson being taught as follows:

> At Coon Rapids Middle School, Jeff Welciek's class pro-gressively occupied half the space in the room until they stood in only one-sixteenth of the space. The activity, which helped them understand increasing population den-sity, illustrates a new math focus on hands-on over com-putation.

One may agree or disagree with teaching that particular theme in our schools, but everyone should agree that the lesson being taught in this math class was really a lesson in civics and government—not mathematics. The new national standards in civics and government require that this kind of nonsense take place.

Similarly, the new textbooks and tests dealing with language arts contain large numbers of selections that are included for the purpose of teaching civics and government. On the reading portion of the national achievement test called the NAEP, for example, there are 15 reading selections—ten of the 15 consist of civics lessons. Even many of the cartoons our nation's children watch during late afternoons and Saturday mornings are now required by federal law to teach civics and government. (See Chapter 5.)

What is "civics education"? Stated simply, civics education is education in citizenship. That is, civics deals with the relationship between citizens and government. When we evaluate the new Federal Curriculum in "civics and government," then, we are studying those themes that are related to government in the United States and how we, as citizens, should be supporting or changing our government.

None of us will argue about the importance of teaching American government and its relationship to its citizens. Indeed, the author of this book is a college professor of American government. He believes that no academic area is more important. The issue of this book, however, is not whether American government should be taught. Not at all. The issues of this book are (1) whether civics and government should be central to the entire curriculum of our schools, (2) whether the curriculum should consist of certain themes instead of academic disciplines, (3) whether the federal government should be dictating the content of this curriculum, (4) whether one NGO should have the sole authority to write this curriculum, (5) whether the content of this curriculum is defensible, and (6) how this new curriculum is being implemented.

As we shall see, the new Federal Curriculum has been developed to dramatically change all of American society, especially American government. As McCune said, the new Federal Curriculum is all about restructuring America. The agenda is not primarily educational, it is primarily ideological and political. We will now further investigate the nature of this new educational and political system.

Chapter Four

Politicizing Education

W hy should civics and government be at the center of the new Federal Curriculum? The reason is this: The new education system is primarily concerned with government, not education. Changing the education system is the means to the ultimate goal, not the goal itself. As will be evident in subsequent chapters, the purpose of the new Federal Curriculum is to mold our children into supporters of a new system of government. Doing so requires that our children be indoctrinated into a worldview that leads to this new form of government. Shirley McCune accurately describes the new Federal Curriculum when she says:

> All learning begins with the affective [attitudes and values]. [and] A major task of education is to extend the **worldview of the child;** this should include **a view of** careers, of the community, our nation and our **global community.** [Emphasis added, *http://www.net/-building/crfut_mccune. html.*]

The Federal Curriculum does include information, of course. It also includes academic subjects that look similar to the academic subjects that have always been taught in our schools. The subjects and the information, however, are peripheral to the new Federal Curriculum. At the core of the new system, as McCune said, is indoctrination into a comprehensive worldview and a clearly identifiable political agenda. Stated simply, the new Federal Curriculum is designed to change the student, not educate the student.

The political agenda of the new Federal Curriculum is evident from the following table which describes the number of times various topics appear in the *National Standards* for *Civics and Government*:

Table 1

Number of Times Various Topics Appear in the National Standards for Civics and Government

References to the environment 17
References to multiculturalism 42
References to the First Amendment 81
References to the Second Amendment 0

Notice the difference in the number of references to the First Amendment to the U.S. Constitution (freedom of religion and speech) as compared to the number of references to the Second Amendment (right to own and bear arms). The national standards contain 81 references to the First Amendment, but no references at all to the Second Amendment. (Later chapters will discuss the topics of environmentalism and multiculturalism.)

How can that kind of difference be explained? The difference becomes even more striking when we observe that federal law (HR6) specifically required the CCE to formulate national standards for teaching our children the Bill of Rights. Isn't the Second Amendment part of the Bill of Rights? (The reader may wish to check the U.S. Constitution to see if the Second Amendment is still there.)

The same view of the Second Amendment is presented in the *Curriculum Standards for Social Studies*, published in 1994 by the National Council for the Social Studies. This curriculum guide contains the following two lists of rights and freedoms under the heading "Democratic Beliefs and Values" (Fourth printing, June, 2001):

A. Rights of the Individual
- Right to life
- Right to liberty
- Right to dignity
- Right to security
- Right to equal opportunity
- Right to justice
- Right to privacy
- Right to private ownership of property

B. Freedoms of the Individual
- Freedom to participate in the political process
- Freedom of worship
- Freedom of thought
- Freedom of conscience
- Freedom of assembly
- Freedom of inquiry
- Freedom of expression [p. 152 of the Standards]

When looking at the above list of rights and freedoms, one again has to ask the question: What happened to the right (or freedom) to own and bear arms? That basic right, once again, is out of sight and out of mind. Its absence is especially conspicuous when one observes that the list of "freedoms" above is merely a restatement of the First Amendment to the Constitution. The First Amendment is referenced seven times, the Second Amendment isn't even referenced once. Why not? The reason is that the Federal Curriculum is about politics, not education.

Lest we forget, the Second Amendment reads as follows:

A well regulated militia, being necessary to the security of a free State, the right of the people to keep and bear arms, shall not be infringed.

The meaning of this amendment is clear enough—that citizens in our land have the constitutional right to keep and bear arms. This amendment is listed second indicating the high priority that it received from those who wrote our Constitution. It is also part of the Bill of Rights which comprise the first ten amendments to the Constitution.

Why, then, does the *National Standards on Civics and Government* fail to include any specific references to the Second Amendment? The national standards omit any and all references to the right to bear arms because the writers of the Federal Curriculum want to eliminate this right.

It is not our purpose here to either defend or assail the right to own and bear arms. Numerous other works take up that task. The point here is merely to observe that the new Federal Curriculum is structured to eliminate the right to bear arms. Out of sight is out of mind. As was mentioned, the new Federal Curriculum is more concerned about attitudes, values and behavior than about teaching accurate information. The Federal Curriculum has no interest in informing students about the Second Amendment and then allowing them to make up their own minds. Not at all. The purpose of the Federal Curriculum is to indoctrinate, not to inform.

The new Federal Curriculum consists of themes, not academic disciplines. As we have just seen, one of the themes of this curriculum is elimination of the right to own and bear arms. This theme, as stated by the platform of The Communitarian Network (the U.S. Department of Education recently established a "partnership" with The Communitarian Network), is as follows:

> There is little sense in gun registration. What we need to enhance public safety is **domestic disarmament**. [Emphasis added, p. 5 of the platform.]

The Communitarians want to eliminate the right to bear arms for all private citizens. According to their platform, only the government should own and bear arms.

The Second Amendment is still part of the Constitution, however. How can the CCE accommodate that fact? On page 207 of the textbook form of the Federal Curriculum, called *We the People: the Citizen and the Constitution*, written by the CCE, is written this statement:

> As fundamental and lasting as its guarantees have been [notice the past tense], the Bill of Rights is a document of the eighteenth century, reflecting the issues and concerns of the age in which it was written.

This postmodernist description of the Bill of Rights suggests that even though the first Ten Amendments to our Constitution were important to the people of the eighteenth century, they may or may not be important today. (Postmodernism holds that knowledge is a mere "social construct," not a matter of truth.) In this way the CCE further weakens the Second Amendment by rewriting (reconstructing) our nation's founding documents and reconstructing our nation's history. The purpose is to make everything conform to the worldview of the CCE. Accurate information is sacrificed for the sake of the themes (ideology) promoted by the CCE.

Further clarification of the procedures of the CCE is included in the introduction in its textbook called *We the People: the Citizen and the Constitution* (1995), which states:

> The primary purpose of this text is not to fill your head with a lot of facts about American history and geography. Knowledge of the facts is important but only insofar as it deepens your understanding of the American Constitutional system and its development [as defined by the CCE]. [p. X]

This statement indicates that the CCE presents only those facts that support its own political viewpoint—any other factual information which is inconsistent with that political agenda is ignored or undermined or both. The program is more about indoctrination than education.

Ironically, the statement above indirectly underscores why it is essential for students to learn a broad range of factual material. How can students decide for themselves what is true and what is important unless they have the basic information, the facts, upon which they can base their own judgments? The new Federal Curriculum, however, has no intention of allowing students to decide for themselves. The new Federal Curriculum has been designed to indoctrinate our nation's children into the ideology of the CCE. The nature of this ideology will be described in greater detail in subsequent chapters.

CHAPTER FIVE

Redefining the Media

Why is the American public unaware of the radical changes that have been taking place in America's system of education? There are several reasons: One of them involves the new role of the media as it relates to the new Federal Curriculum. For example, the UN sponsored World Declaration on Education for All, 1990, which called for most of the education changes that are being made in the United States, made the following statement:

> [Promoting the new education system] means capitalizing on the use of traditional and modern information media and technologies to educate the public on matters of social concern and to **support** basic education activities. [Emphasis added, *http://www2.unesco.org/eta/07/bpubl.htm*, p. 5.]

That is, nations signing this policy declaration (as did President George Bush, Sr.) agreed to employ the media to "support" the new program. Is that the proper role of the media? Should it **support** the new system, or should it **report** on the system? There is a difference. Traditionally, America's media has seen itself as having the responsibility to "report" on the news, not to "support" it. The media, obviously, cannot do both at the same time without compromising one or the other roles.

The world-wide environmental compact known as Agenda 21 also views the media this way. Agenda 21, moreover, adds additional explanation. It states:

> Countries and the United Nations system should promote a **cooperative relationship** with the media...to mobilize their experience in **shaping public behavior**. [Emphasis added, Section 31:10.]

The media are to support the goals described in various international agreements. Does that mean "reporting" to the public? Not at all. It means, in the words of Agenda 21, "shaping public behavior." In other words, the media is now engaged in propaganda, not objective information.

Margaret Stimmann Branson, Associate Director of the Center for Civic Education, described the new role of the media the same way. She said:

> ...the media are important influences and have significant contributions to make to civic education, and their **support** should be enlisted. [Stimmann Branson's emphasis, http://civiced.org.//articles_role.html.]

Stimmann Branson is echoing the words of the World Declaration as she, too, says the media are now to "support" the new Curriculum. It would be difficult to overemphasize the difference between the words "report" and "support." Maybe it's time the American public knew what the media are up to. The implications of this new role of the media are profound.

How does the media "support" the new system? One telling illustration involves the right to bear arms issue as described in Chapter 4.

As was demonstrated, the new Federal Curriculum intends to eliminate this Second Amendment right. How does the media "support" that political position?

John Lott, Jr., Senior Researcher at Yale Law School, explains one way the media play that role as he gives the following factual account: On October 11, 1997, two students were shot to death by a fellow student at a high school in Mississippi. The assistant principal, when he saw what was happening, ran to his car, grabbed a handgun, ran back into the school and, pointing the handgun at the assailant, subdued him until the police arrived some time later.

How did the media "report" the beneficial use of a gun which was a significant part of this incident? Lott determined that over 700 media outlets carried the story of the school shooting, but how many of these media outlets reported the positive use of a gun? Lott's findings are summarized on the following table:

Table 2
Number of Times Media Outlets Mentioned the
Beneficial Use of a Gun

- Only 19 media outlets even mentioned the assistant principal.
- Only 13 media outlets reported that the assistant principal played a significant role.
- Only 9 media outlets indicated that the assistant principal had or used a gun.

[Speech delivered by John Lott, Jr. at the Council for National Policy, 7-27-2000.]

As is obvious from the above table, the media were more interested in "supporting" a particular political position—eliminating our Second Amendment rights—than in "reporting" the news in an accurate fashion. (If people know that guns are usually used for good purposes, they are less likely to support the elimination of the right to bear arms.)

A similar case in point occurred in the summer of 2001 and involved the following Associated Press news story as printed in the Minneapolis *Star Tribune* newspaper. The story read as follows:

PENSACOLA, FLA.—An 8-year old boy attacked by a shark over the weekend suffered harm to virtually every organ because of blood loss and may have brain damage, a doctor said Monday.

Jessie Arbogast's arm—reattached after it was pried out of a shark's mouth and delivered to surgeons—was healing well. But the boy remained in critical condition Monday after at least six operations to repair damage from Friday night's attack....

The Ocean Springs, Miss., boy was attacked at the Gulf Islands National Seashore in the Florida Panhandle.

His uncle, Vance Flosenzier of Mobile, Ala., wrestled the 7-foot bull shark to shore with the help of another beach-goer, said the spokeswoman Megan MacPherson. She said Flosenzier did not want to release any information about himself and he did not know who helped him.

How, then, did the bystanders manage to pry the boy's arm out of the shark's mouth? Most Americans never found out because most media accounts, like the one above, refused to say. The answer to that question is that an individual at the beach used a handgun to shoot the shark between the eyes so that its mouth could be pried open and the boy's arm could then be retrieved from the shark's throat.

Once again, the media chose to give American citizens an incomplete account of the event rather than mention that a firearm had been used in a positive way. Once again, the media chose to "support" the political agenda of the new Federal Curriculum, rather than accurately "report" the news.

Another way the news media supports the new Federal Curriculum is by including the Curriculum in its programming. In meeting the agreement stated in the "World Declaration for Education for All," Congress passed the Children's Television Act (CTA), also in 1990. As enforced by the Federal Communications Commission (FCC), this act requires all television stations to air at least three hours of programming that will, according to the FCC, "serve the educational and information needs of children," (http://www.fcc.gov). That is, three hours of broadcast must teach the new Federal Curriculum in some way.

One such show, as listed by the FCC, is a Disney production called *Recess*. KMSP Television (Twin Cities area, Minnesota) commonly airs this show in late afternoons on weekdays, as well as Sunday mornings, so it can be seen both by preschool and school-age children. Other networks typically air the show on Saturday and Sunday mornings. *Recess* provides lessons in "character education" where each 12-minute drama ends with a "moral" of some kind. Typical lessons are, "You have to face your fears directly," "Don't give up," and "You guys were there when I needed you." On the negative side, the teacher in the show, "Miss Spinster," is pictured as mean, ugly and highly sadistic. (The new Federal Curriculum takes a dim view of teachers, who are seen and described as being "facilitators," not "instructors" or "educators.")

One may be supportive or critical of the kind of character education taking place on network TV, but that is not the question at hand. For now we will simply observe that teaching attitudes and values is central to the new Federal Curriculum, and all TV stations are now required by law to air three hours of "educational" programming each week. These programs must meet the approval of the Federal Communications Commission. Even though the values being taught on these programs appear to be both superficial and benign, the implications are, nonetheless, very profound. The news media is now required by law to "support" the new Federal Curriculum.

CHAPTER SIX

Bringing in Private and Home Schools

T he new education system has always said that it would encompass all students, including private school and home school students. For example, the Goals 2000 law passed in 1994 contains numerous statements like the following:

Goal 3 Student Achievement and Citizenship
By the year 2000, all students will leave grades 4, 8, and 12 having demonstrated competency over challenging subject matter including...civics and government.

Notice the words "all students." In the new education system, "all students" means all students, including private school and home school students. How will these non-public students be brought into the new program? This is the way it will work: As stated by the *National Standards for Civics and Government*, these national standards will form the basis for "textbooks, professional development programs, and systems of assessments." That is exactly what has happened. In December of 2001, for example, the author received a brochure from W. W. Norton & Company, Inc., advertising its new textbook on American government called *Essentials of American Politics*. The first statement made about this text in the brochure, in large blue letters, was:

> Based on the acclaimed *We the People*, Third Edition, [*www.wwnorton.com/college/polisci*].

What is *We the People*, Third Edition? It's the textbook form of the new Federal Curriculum, written by the Center for Civic Education (CCE). Notice the words "based on." The brochure didn't say "influenced by"; it said, "Based on...*We the People*." That statement makes it clear that this textbook has been designed for the specific purpose of teaching the new Federal Curriculum.

Why would a college-level textbook be based on the new Federal Curriculum? College classes and textbooks are under no legal obligation to teach this Curriculum. Why would publishers have books written, and promoted, as being based on the Federal Curriculum? It is because the new education system is in the process of having all significant tests rewritten to conform to the new Federal Curriculum. For example, testing expert, Dr. George Cunningham of Louisville, Kentucky, described the revised form of a widely used aptitude test for teachers as follows:

> Last week I went to a workshop on PRAXIS, the teacher aptitude test administered in 38 states.... Many of the sample questions we were given could be answered by simply picking the most politically correct answer.

In other words, the questions would be answered correctly by those who had been schooled in the political agenda of the new Federal Curriculum. Cunningham also said:

> Every standardized test must be approved, item by item, by diversity/sensitivity committees.... Not only can no item cast aspersions on any protected group, no item can fail to put them in the most favorable light. The problem

with this is that if you want your students to perform well, they must be indoctrinated with this point of view.

As we shall see in Chapter 12, diversity is only one of the themes required by the new Federal Curriculum. High schools look at testing the same way, of course. For example, the Islamic curriculum now taught in many California schools is being defended as follows (as described by World Net Daily, Jan. 11, 2002):

> Adams [the curriculum director] also stresses the state guidelines and standards "are not mandatory," and the state recognized the need for local control within school districts. Asked whether Byron [the school] would exercise local control and opt out of the Islam studies, Castro [the superintendent] replied, "The state tests our students and ranks our performance on this curriculum. If we didn't teach parts of it, students would not succeed in achieving the standards."

Similarly, if private school and home school students are not taught the new curriculum, they will be at a substantial disadvantage when taking the important tests. It used to be that private and home school students did much better than their public school counterparts on both achievement tests and aptitude tests, the reason being that non-public school students generally had better skills in reading, math and science than their public school counterparts. Non-public school students have also possessed greater knowledge in the academic disciplines.

That superior performance by non-public school students will soon come to an end because all tests will be redesigned to measure only what students have learned as specified by state standards. These state standards, in turn, are closely tied to the new Federal Curriculum.

The question for all schools, including non-public schools, will be: Do you want your student to do well on the tests? Do you want them to do well on the ACT test, or the SAT test, or the Iowa Basics test?" How about the Graduate Record Exam which is often required to be admitted to graduate school?

The new Federal Curriculum is structured to discriminate against those students who do not comply with the new standards. As a consequence, non-public school students will be largely prevented from becoming tomorrow's leaders unless they are taught the new Federal Curriculum. Who will tomorrow's teachers be? Who will the attorneys be? Who will the medical doctors be? The system is structured to screen out any students who have not been schooled in the new Federal Curriculum.

CHAPTER SEVEN

Defining the
Curriculum as Themes

In a sense there has always been a Federal Curriculum. Twenty years ago a family could travel to any state in the nation and the children in that family would enroll in pretty much the same subjects. They would study mathematics, reading, literature, history, geography, science, government and the like. In that sense, a national curriculum has existed in our nation for a long time.

What, then, has changed? The first change is that prior to the federal laws passed in 1994, the national curriculum existed by common consent of the schools and by decisions of state governments, not by federal law. In 1994 the federal government made itself the highest authority over the curriculum in the schools. (See Chapter 2.)

The second change is that the new curriculum requirements of the federal government consist of both academic and theme requirements involving attitudes, values and beliefs (worldview). The worldview portion of the Federal Curriculum is the most significant part. For example, the new Federal Curriculum in civics and government requires all schools to teach students the American Constitution including the

Bill of Rights. Schools, however, have always taught the Constitution and the Bill of Rights. What is new or important about that?

The significance of the federal requirements is that schools are now required to teach, not just the subjects of the Constitution and the Bill of Rights, but also particular attitudes (themes) regarding the Constitution and the Bill of Rights. For example, "The Second Amendment" is an academic subject that should be taught in any course in American government. In contrast, "eliminating the Second Amendment," is a theme (or attitude) that is part of the Federal Curriculum. The Federal Curriculum is clearly more interested in teaching the theme then in teaching the subject.

Along this line, the *National Standards for Civics and Government* says: "[Student] participation requires the acquisition of a body of knowledge and...certain dispositions or traits of character...." The "certain dispositions or traits of character" (attitudes) required are the most important part of the new Federal Curriculum.

What are the required themes of the new Federal Curriculum? That question cannot be answered by reproducing a straightforward and comprehensive statement made by the Federal Curriculum itself. The Federal Curriculum fails to provide such a statement. (The reason for this failure will become obvious as we proceed.) That does not mean, however, that the required themes are difficult to determine or describe. The themes are really quite obvious. The new curriculum can be defined by reading the primary source documents while asking the question, "What themes, specifically, is this curriculum requiring that our children be taught?"

As was noted earlier, the civics and government curriculum forms the heart and center of the new Federal Curriculum. The civics and government curriculum is the core curriculum. For that reason, the book, *National Standards for Civics and Government*, is the most important source for determining what the requirements of the new Federal Curriculum actually are. This book was written at the direction of federal law in 1994 to describe the standards for civics and government which make up the core of the new Federal Curriculum. This book provides the principal source material for the chapters that follow.

Once the significance and nature of the *National Standards for Civics and Government* has been recognized, the task of describing its curriculum requirements is relatively simple and straightforward. The content of this curriculum is summarized by the following list of seven themes. There may be some room for discussion and debate regarding the exact wording and organization of this list. At the same time, however, there is little room for doubt that the following themes are required by the New Federal Curriculum.

The principal themes required by the new Federal Curriculum are:

1. Undermining national sovereignty.
2. Redefining natural rights.
3. Minimizing natural law.
4. Promoting environmentalism.
5. Requiring multiculturalism.
6. Restructuring government.
7. Redefining education as job skills

Notice that the Federal Curriculum is stated, not merely as subjects, but also as themes (or attitudes). That is how it must be stated because the curriculum requires both subjects and attitudes. In addition, the significance of the new Federal Curriculum lies primarily in the attitudes (worldview) that it requires. The subjects are mere window dressing for the required themes.

There can be no doubt that the new Federal Curriculum does mandate the teaching of attitudes. For example, in describing the requirements for educational TV that all networks must now broadcast, the Federal Communications Commission stated that the purpose of these federal requirements was to teach "information, skills, values, and behavior" [August 8, 1996, *http://www.fcc.gov*].

How can we know that this list of themes stated above is an accurate description of the new Federal Curriculum? The reason we know that the above list is accurate is because this curriculum is contained in all the major documents. As stated above, this new Federal Curriculum is contained in the *National Standards for Civics and Government.* That book will be the principal source utilized in the subsequent chapters. The themes are also evident in the federal government's one achievement test called the NAEP (National Assessment of Educational Progress).

They are additionally now contained in the other national achievement tests, such as the Iowa Test of Basic Skills, and are included in the nationwide textbooks as stated above in *Essentials of American Politics.* (These textbooks and tests have been rewritten since 1994 when the federal government took over education policy in our country.)

The new Federal Curriculum is also contained in the World Declaration on Education for All, 1990, agreed to by then President George Bush, Sr. In whatever primary source we investigate, we find the new Federal Curriculum. In each of these sources, the basic content of the Curriculum is the same.

We now turn to the seven themes which will be discussed one area and one chapter at a time. In each of these subsequent chapters, it will be demonstrated that the new Federal Curriculum does, in fact, require that this theme be taught in our schools.

PART II

The Content of the
New Federal Curriculum

Chapter Eight

Undermining National Sovereignty

The new Federal Curriculum is a program of "out with the old, in with the new." The "old" governmental principles that must go are national sovereignty, natural rights and natural law. The "new" governmental values now required by the Federal Curriculum consist of environmentalism, multiculturalism, restructuring government, and redefining education as job skills.

As was mentioned, the new Federal Curriculum consists, not only of academic information, but also of a clearly defined worldview. For that reason, each learning area contains more than a subject; it includes a political position on that subject. The first learning area, accordingly, is not merely "national sovereignty"; it's really that of "undermining national sovereignty." A curriculum can study national sovereignty objectively, or it can promote a theme regarding national sovereignty which will either undermine it or support it. As we shall see, the new Federal Curriculum is designed to undermine national sovereignty.

The first method the Federal Curriculum uses to undermine national sovereignty is that of minimizing it. Consider the following table, based on the *National Standards for Civics and Government*, as the table compares the number of entries in the standards on several subjects:

Table 3
Number of References to Selected Subjects in the New Standards

References to the environment 17
References to multiculturalism 42
References to the 1st Amendment 81
References to national sovereignty 8

In the 137 pages of text that make up the new *National Standards in Civics and Government*, there are eight references to national sovereignty. Obviously, environmentalism and multiculturalism are considered to be more important than national sovereignty.

Even more striking, however, is a list of the so-called "fundamental values" of the United States as printed by the CCE in "CIVITAS: a Framework for Civic Education." The list reads as follows:

1. The public good.
2. Individual rights.
3. Justice.
4. Equality.
5. Diversity.
6. Truth.
7. Patriotism.

This list of "fundamental values" leaves much to be desired. The point here, however, is that national sovereignty didn't even make the list!

Does the list above reflect the view our nation's founders had of national sovereignty? On the contrary, our forefathers made it clear that national sovereignty is one of the most fundamental principles of our nation. In the Declaration of Independence, for example, they said (in the very first paragraph):

48

When in the Course of human Events, it becomes necessary for one People to dissolve the Political Bands which
have connected them with another, and to assume among
the Powers of the Earth, the separate and equal Station to
which the Laws of Nature and of Nature's God entitle
them....

In the last paragraph of the Declaration of Independence the
founders said:

We, therefore, the Representatives of the UNITED
STATES OF AMERICA...do Declare that these United
Colonies are, and of Right ought to be, Free and
Independent States...they have full Power to levy War,
conclude Peace, contract Alliances, establish Commerce,
and do all other Acts and Things which Independent
States may of right do.

The Declaration of Independence begins and ends with an affir-
mation of national sovereignty. That is how important national sovereignty was to our founding fathers. The architects of our free country
insisted that the United States ought to be, and is, an independent,
free, sovereign nation. It is difficult to imagine how our forefathers
could have emphasized national sovereignty any more than they actually did in the Declaration. (We should also recognize that the
Declaration of Independence states that our nation was constructed
on three fundamental principles. The first one listed is national sovereignty. The other two are natural rights and natural law. The next two
chapters will describe how the new Federal Curriculum weakens the
other two fundamental principles.)

Even more important than minimizing national sovereignty, however, is the manner by which the Federal Curriculum treats this criti-
cally important principle. As was described in the above table, national
sovereignty is mentioned eight times in the *National Standards for Civics
and Government*. On two of those occasions, the subject is mentioned
in passing in sidebar quotations, and no explanation of the subject is
given. The other six times national sovereignty is mentioned, however,

it is mentioned in the main text and is worded exactly the same way. (Writers normally use a variety of words and approaches to describe a principle. The fact that the wording on national sovereignty is exactly the same on all six occasions is highly significant. It demonstrates that this wording has been constructed with great care and is very important.) That wording is as follows:

> The world is divided into nation-states that claim sovereignty over a defined territory and jurisdiction over everyone within it. [P. 121 of the *National Standards on Civics and Government*.]

Notice the wording, "The world is divided into...." The language should read, "The world consists of," which would then be accurate. If, however, it is accurate to say that "the world is divided into," then what is, or should be, the primary political unit? The entire world, of course. The world becomes the primary political entity, and the nations become mere pieces of the whole. The nations become secondary.

For example, we could correctly say that our nation is divided into 50 states. That is an accurate statement because the federal government is the larger political unit which has greater authority than any of the states. When the new Federal Curriculum says, "The world is divided into nation-states that claim sovereignty...," it implies that a world political unit should have greater power and authority than any of the nations, including the United States of America. Such a worldwide political power would be a one-world government, of course.

This "the world is divided into nation-states" language can be compared to the way we view an apple pie. It's like asking the question, "How many pieces would you like this pie cut into?" With regard to pies, the language is accurate because the pie is the whole entity; the pieces are mere parts of the whole. Nations, in contrast, are complete entities by themselves, not mere parts of the whole.

If we were to describe, using the pie analogy, a class of kindergarten students, we would say, "This class is divided into 22 students." We don't speak that way, of course; but why not? The reason is that each student is an independent entity that is far more important than just being one portion of a kindergarten class. The same principle holds true in the relationship between nations and the rest of the world. Nations are more than pieces of the world; they are complete, independent entities in their own right.

Notice also the language, "*claim* sovereignty." The United States has been a sovereign nation for over two hundred years. Is that all we can say about our nation that it has a "*claim*" to sovereignty? Shouldn't we boldly say that we are a sovereign nation? That is what we said in The Declaration of Independence at a time when our national sovereignty was certainly more open to question than it is today.

Would a prosecuting attorney in a murder case say that the injured party "claimed" to have a right to life. Wouldn't the attorney act on the assumption that the person did, in fact, have this right to life? Wouldn't the defense attorney agree with that assumption? How likely would it be for a defense attorney to suggest that a murdered person merely "claimed" to have a right to life? A jury would, of course, reject such an absurd suggestion.

That kind of suggestion, however, is exactly the implication made by the new Federal Curriculum when it repeatedly says that nations *claim* sovereignty. The wording implies that this national sovereignty is subject to question, that it should not be assumed to be real or legitimate.

We should also observe that the wording used to describe national sovereignty in the new Federal Curriculum follows the same cutting-the-apple-pie form used in the *Humanist Manifesto II*. The *Manifesto* says:

> We deplore the **division of humankind on nationalistic grounds**. We have reached a turning point in human history where the best option is to transcend the limits of national sovereignty and to move toward the building of a world community...based upon a **transnational federal government**. [Emphasis added.]

Notice the similarity of wording in the two documents. The *Humanist Manifesto II* says "the division of humankind on nationalistic grounds," while the *National Standards* say "the world is divided into nation-states." The conceptual framework is the same. We know why the *Humanist Manifesto* is worded as it is—the *Manifesto* advocates the replacement of national sovereignty with a one-world government. By its similar language, the Federal Curriculum implies the same objective.

Words are important. They contain great power. The new Federal Standards are worded with great care. The wording of these standards needs to be taken seriously.

Chapter Nine

Redefining Natural Rights

As was mentioned in Chapter 6, the United States of America was founded on three fundamental principles. Those three principles are (1) national sovereignty, (2) natural rights, and (3) natural law. We have seen how the new Federal Curriculum undermines national sovereignty. We now turn to the matter of natural rights.

We will begin with the natural rights contained in the first Ten Amendments to the United States Constitution, also known as the Bill of Rights. As we saw in Chapter 2, the federal law passed in 1994, HR6, empowered the Center for Civic Education to write the national standards for teaching the Bill of Rights. What do these standards look like? Are they primarily academic, or are they largely political?

That question is answered by the CCE's middle school textbook called *We the People*. The top of page ii of this textbook appears as follows:

Directed by the
Center for Civic Education
and
Funded by the
U.S. Department of Education by act of Congress
Established 1987 under the
Commission on the Bicentennial of the
United States Constitution

As can be seen, this CCE textbook on American government was funded by the taxpayers, was authorized by an act of Congress, and was part of our bicentennial celebration. Clearly, this textbook has an official air about it. The book was written at considerable expense and with great care. This middle school textbook has a section called the "Bill of Rights." This is how the main part of this section reads:

> The Bill of Rights was passed by the first Congress. It contains ten amendments. The first eight list basic protections that had already been guaranteed in most of the state constitutions. Some of the most important of these include:
>
> * freedom of religion
> * freedom of the press
> * freedom of speech
> * the rights of assembly and petition
> * the right to a speedy, public trial by jury
>
> The Ninth Amendment states that the listing of certain rights does not mean that these are the only rights the people have. Finally, the Tenth Amendment states that the powers not given to the federal government by the Constitution, nor forbidden by the Constitution to the states, belong to the states or the people.

Notice the "sleight-of-hand" trick in this account. The wording is designed to give the impression that a reasonably accurate and comprehensive list of the Bill of Rights is included in this section. If so, whatever happened to the Second Amendment right to own and bear arms? Look again at the wording. It never claims to give a balanced, objective, fair or comprehensive list. It only claims to list "some of the most important" rights. Who determines which "important" rights will make the list? The CCE, of course. The textbook left the door open to omit any basic right it wishes to omit.

This type of treatment of the Bill of Rights is totally misleading. How many middle school students will see through this kind of deception? Close to none. How many teachers will see through it? Not very many.

Why mislead people this way? The reason is those who have designed the new Federal Curriculum know full well that the public would not accept the new curriculum if it were presented in an open and honest manner. Everything must be presented in a misleading fashion in order to disguise the real nature of the curriculum. If the new Federal Curriculum is ever exposed to the light of day, it will be rejected by the American people.

That is why the Second Amendment to the Constitution is usually not attacked directly. It is dealt with instead by being "out of sight and out of mind" in the new Federal Curriculum. The Second Amendment must be undermined, however, the reason being that disarming the American citizenry is one of the top objectives of the one-world government crowd. They know that the American public will resist the one-world tyranny if they have a means to do so. Once again, the new Federal Curriculum is far more interested in teaching its particular ideology to our children than in providing reasonably accurate and objective standards. The new Federal Curriculum is indoctrination disguised as education.

In direct contrast to the new national standards, the framers of our nation made it abundantly clear that this new nation was based on the proper recognition of all the natural rights. In paragraph 2 of the Declaration of Independence, they said:

> We hold these truths to be self-evident, that all men are created equal, that they have been endowed by their Creator with certain unalienable Rights, that among these are Life, Liberty and the pursuit of Happiness. That to secure these rights, Governments are instituted among Men....

Notice that the Declaration states that the reality of natural rights is a matter of "truths" that are "self-evident." Notice that the Declaration says we have been given these natural rights by our Creator God. Notice that these rights are described as being "unalienable." Notice that the natural rights are said to include life, liberty and the pursuit of happiness (private property). Notice, most of all, that the primary purpose of government is described by the Declaration as that of protecting these natural rights of life, liberty and property.

In the Declaration of Independence, also, the words were chosen with great care. In the Declaration, the words chosen outlined the most fundamental difference between freedom and tyranny. That is, in a free society the natural rights must be "unalienable." Protecting the rights of its people to life, liberty and property must be the first priority of the government. In a totalitarian state, in contrast, protection of the basic rights of life, liberty and property have a position lower than priority one.

To give a very graphic example, the constitution of the former Soviet Union said that Soviet citizens had most of the same rights that we Americans enjoy. At the same time, however, the Soviet Constitution also said human rights were secondary to the primary purpose of the Soviet Government, namely, creating the worldwide Communist utopia envisioned by Karl Marx. The utopian vision (good of society) was number one, individual human rights were number two. For that reason, Joseph Stalin and others could, for example, defend the murder of 50 million Soviet citizens on the ground that it was necessary for the good of the Soviet State and its ultimate goals. (Later Soviet leaders referred to the "excesses" of Stalin, but they never disputed the overall principle that human rights were secondary to the interests of the Soviet State.)

Protecting the natural rights of life, liberty and property will be the top priority of government in a free society. Protecting our natural rights is goal number one. Otherwise the natural rights mean nothing at all. Natural rights are not rights if they can be sacrificed for some supposed greater good. The architects of our nation understood this principle clearly. They said the natural rights are "unalienable." They said the protection of these rights is the primary purpose of government.

Margaret Stimmann Branson, Associate Director of the Center for Civic Education, made it clear that she understands exactly how this works. In a speech she gave several years ago, she said:

> First let's look at the conception of rights on which the U.S. Constitution is based and how and why that conception has been exported to, accepted and modified by many nations throughout the world..... These rights are preexisting, inalienable, entitlements. [*http://www.civiced.org/rights.html*, pp. 1 & 2]

In this speech, Stimman Branson quoted the Declaration of Independence pointing out that in America these rights are seen as being God-given. In the United States, she said, the primary purpose of government is to protect these natural rights.

She then continued her speech by saying:

> Secondly, let's consider rights as they are conceived in the constitutions of the Communist world.... [As stated by the constitution of Cuba, for example] "Citizens have freedom of speech in keeping with the goals of the socialist society." [p. 1]

Once again, Stimmann Branson was correct in describing the view of natural rights in Communist countries. In these totalitarian states, human rights have second priority, not first. The "needs of society" (as stated in the 1977 Soviet Constitution) have the top priority. When human rights are given second place in government, as they are in Communist countries, they cease to mean anything at all.

We now come to the critical issue. We have seen how free countries define natural human rights. We have also seen how Communist countries define natural human rights. There is, however, a third view—the internationalist view. Stimmann Branson also defined this view as she continued her speech. She said:

> Finally, we'll focus briefly on American attitudes toward the Universal Declaration of Human Rights which

attempts to **combine the competing conceptions.**
[Emphasis added, p. 1.]

Stimmann Branson was, once again, accurate in what she said.
This third view, the internationalist view, as contained in the UN's
Universal Declaration of Human Rights, combines (synthesizes) the
other two views. What was the reason for combining the two different
views of human rights? The reason was that the Universal Declaration
of Human Rights was constructed to be acceptable to the Communist
countries. That kind of combination is like mixing oil and water, of
course. It doesn't work. But that is also why the Communist countries
were quick to ratify the Declaration. That is also why the United
States refused to ratify the Universal Declaration of Human Rights.
Trying to mix the human rights view of the free world with the
Communist view of human rights will always end up being the
Communist view (see Chapter 15). Either protecting the natural
human rights is the top priority of government, or the natural human
rights mean nothing at all.

Which view of the natural human rights is promoted by the new
Federal Curriculum? Can we assume that the Federal Curriculum
teaches the American viewpoint? Guess again. The new Federal
Curriculum, without reservation, advocates the internationalist view.
The National Standards for Civics and Government says:

Explain that the **purposes** of government in the United
States are to protect the rights of individuals **and** to promote the common good. [Emphasis added, p. 17.]

Notice the parallel construction. Protecting the human rights and
promoting the common good (which government can define to mean
anything it wishes it to mean) are placed on the same level in the new
standards. This is the internationalist view of human rights as defined
by the Universal Declaration of Human Rights. It is not the American
view. The new Federal Curriculum rejects the American position on
human rights and embraces the internationalist view instead. Federal
law now requires that this internationalist (and Communist) view be
taught to our children.

The *National Standards for Civics and Government* further undermines the natural rights by contending that our nation exists in a constant tension between the two views of human rights. The one view, that of our forefathers, the *Standards* describes as follows:

> They argued that the principal purpose of government is the protection of individual rights, the "unalienable rights to life liberty and the pursuit of happiness," of which Jefferson spoke in the Declaration of Independence. [p. 8]

If this were the view actually being promoted by the new Federal Curriculum, we could say that the Curriculum is faithful to our nation's history and also to our foundational principles. Sadly, such is not the case. The *Standards* also states that the view of our founders, as described above, is only equal to the following view:

> [Another view is] that the primary purpose of government is to promote the common good of the whole society rather than that of one particular class or segment of society. [p. 8]

Although this approach to human rights is stated in nice sounding language, it is, nonetheless, the internationalist and Communist view. This is "historical revisionism" at its worst. The United States of America lives by the principle that protecting the natural human rights is the first function of government. The good of society comes second. This has always been the guiding principle of our nation. This is the only way freedom can function.

The CCE further weakens the natural rights by its description of natural rights in its model textbook, *We the People: the Citizen and the Constitution*, which states:

> As fundamental and lasting as its guarantees have been [notice the past tense], the U.S. Bill of Rights is a document of the eighteenth century, reflecting the issues and concerns of the age in which it was written.... Other national guarantees of rights also reflect the cultures that created them. [p. 207]

In other words, then was then and now is now. The implication of this statement is that the doctrine of natural rights may have been fine for the eighteenth century, but we are more enlightened now. This is a classic statement of postmodern ideology—meaning that statements like the Bill of Rights are merely products of the cultures that created them (see Chapter 12). Since, to the postmodernist, no culture is superior to any other, and since other cultures look at rights differently, the Bill of Rights is just one option among many in the worldwide smorgasbord of values. We may happen to like the idea of natural rights, but it is just a cultural preference, nothing more.

The Federal Curriculum further weakens the natural rights at the very end of the *National Standards for Civics and Government*. The second to the last paragraph says:

> Explain how awareness of the nature of American constitutional democracy may give citizens the ability to reaffirm or **change** fundamental constitutional values. [Emphasis added, p. 137.]

What does it mean to "change fundamental constitutional values"? The Declaration of Independence says that the natural rights are God-given and "unalienable." That means unchangeable. In contrast, the Federal Curriculum says we can now "change fundamental constitutional values." We cannot have it both ways. Either our foundational values are God-given, "self-evident" and "unalienable," or they are not. Can we change (or eliminate) the right to life? Can we eliminate personal liberty? Can we eliminate the right to private property? Can we eliminate the freedom of speech? Can we rid ourselves of the right to own and bear arms? Sure, we can do any of these things, but we cease to be a free people if we do. Is that what the new Federal Curriculum has in mind? Yes, it is.

(See Chapters 4 and 5 for an analysis of how the new Federal Curriculum eliminates the Second Amendment right to own and bears arms.)

CHAPTER TEN

Minimizing Natural Law

As was mentioned earlier, our nation was founded on three fundamental principles. Those three principles are national sovereignty, natural rights and natural law. We now turn our attention to natural law. The Declaration of Independence, once again, says:

> When in the course of human events it becomes necessary for one people to dissolve the political bands which have connected them with another, and to assume, among the powers of the earth, the separate and equal station to which the **Laws of Nature** and of **Nature's God** entitle them, a decent respect to the opinions of mankind requires that they should declare the causes which impel them to the separation. [Emphasis added.]

As can be seen by the above quotation, the colonists said that they were entitled to form a new and separate nation based upon the "Laws of Nature and of Nature's God," a principle known as "natural law." The

Declaration also makes it clear that "natural rights" are the result of this natural law ("all men...are endowed by their Creator with certain unalienable rights").

What is natural law? A college-level textbook, *American Government: Roots and Reform* (1993 Edition), correctly described natural law as follows:

> Where Did our Ideas of Government Come From?
> ...classical and medieval theorists such as St. Thomas Aquinas (1225-1274) argued that...governments were ordained by **natural law**—basic and God-given rules that do not have to be written down so much as discovered. Individual rights to life and liberty were a part of this natural law created by God. (p. 6)

As this pre-1994 textbook clarified, the natural rights (see Chapter 8) are a result of natural law—universal standards of right and wrong that apply to all people and all governments. Why, for example, do people have a right to life? The reason is that our Creator God established universal moral principles, one of them being the right to life. And why is murder wrong? Because every person has a right to live. Why is theft wrong? Because every person has a God-given right to own property. Natural rights and natural law are two sides of the same coin. You cannot have one without the other. Our nation was founded on both principles—along with the third principle of national sovereignty.

One would hope that a principle as important as natural law would receive adequate recognition in the *National Standards for Civics and Government*. Unfortunately, such is not the case. The following table describes the frequency of appearance in the *National Standards* of certain topics:

Table 4
Number of References to Various Topics in the New Standards

References to the environment 17
References to diversity 42

As can be seen, natural law made the standards, but just barely. Students quickly identify what is important and what is not, of course. Something mentioned only once in 137 pages is not going to be viewed as very important.

In addition to minimizing natural law, the *National Standards for Civics and Government* make several statements like the following:

> Americans have been affected by the political ideas of other nations from the ideas of the natural rights philosophers...to ideas about social and economic rights such as those found in the Universal Declaration of Human Rights. [p. 73]

The implication of this postmodernist statement is that America borrowed its views on natural rights (based on natural law) from certain philosophers of the past, and we now borrow ideas about basic rights from international accords. The one is presented as being no better than the other—even though our nation was founded on natural rights and natural law, not on international agreements.

Once again, we can't have it both ways. If natural law is to be meaningful, then it is true and absolute. To treat natural law and natural rights as just one philosophical option among many choices is to minimize natural law and natural rights to the point of their being virtually meaningless. This kind of treatment of natural law and natural rights by the new National Curriculum is indefensible.

As was said earlier, our nation was founded on the three principles of national sovereignty, natural rights, and natural law. The new standards have minimized and undermined all three. As was also said earlier, the new Federal Curriculum is a matter of "out with the old, in with the new." Having seen how the Federal Curriculum has dismissed the basic principles that formed the foundation of our free nation, we now examine the new values that are being instituted in their place.

CHAPTER ELEVEN

Promoting Environmentalism

It is no overstatement to say that the new Federal Curriculum requires the teaching of environmentalism. For example, the *National Standards for Civics and Government* includes numerous requirements like the following:

> ...describe principal environmental conditions that affect the United States, e.g. destruction of rain forests, air pollution, water pollution...[p. 125]

Most Americans, including the author, consider themselves to be environmentalists. Most Americans, including the author, will not object to environmentalism being taught in the schools. Most Americans will want their children to know the important facts about environmental issues.

There are numerous problems associated with the new Federal Curriculum's mandate for environmental education, however. As this requirement is played out in the classroom, textbooks, and national tests; it carries with it a clearly identifiable, and radical, worldview agenda. This agenda may be summarized by the following three observations: (1) The environmentalism in the Federal Curriculum is exaggerated in comparison to other concerns. (2) The environmentalism in the Federal Curriculum includes the teaching of an identifiable religion. (3) The environmentalism in the Federal Curriculum has major implications for a restructuring of our form of government. We will consider each of these three issues, one at a time.

EXAGGERATED ENVIRONMENTALISM

As was pointed out in previous chapters, the new Federal Curriculum has far more references to protecting the environment than to most other concerns, such as national sovereignty. At the same time, the manner in which national sovereignty was treated by the National Curriculum also implied that such sovereignty is of questionable value. Does that suggest that environmental protection is more important than national sovereignty? The following table will answer that question.

Especially significant is the emphasis placed on environmentalism in national tests and textbooks written after 1994 and which are now based on the new Federal Curriculum. In the Social Studies section of the 6th grade Iowa Basics Test, for example, there are a total of 42 questions. Twelve of these 42 questions deal with environmental issues. That is, 29% of the social studies test questions in this Iowa Basics Test deal with the environment. If we compare those 12 environmental questions on the Iowa Basics to other topics that should be of importance, this is what we find:

Table 5
Number of Questions on Various Subjects in the Iowa Basics Test

The United States Constitution 0
Any United States President 0
Any explorer such as Christopher Columbus 0
Any United States leader 0
Any of the wars involving the United States 0

The basic rights of life, liberty, or property. 0
The importance of free enterprise. 0
The meaning of being a democracy or republic 0
The location of any state, any river, any city,
any territory, any ocean or any nation 0
The environment 12

Assuming that teachers and schools want their students to do well on the Iowa Basics Test, will they spend more time on basic facts of American history, geography, and government, or will they spend more time on environmental issues? The answer to that question is obvious from the table.

Also significant is the emphasis on environmentalism in the federal government's own achievement test, the NAEP (National Assessment of Educational Progress), as compared to other values. That comparison is summarized in the table below (on the 8th grade level test):

Table 6
NAEP Questions on Environmentalism Compared to Questions on other Values

NAEP questions dealing with
protection of the environment 10
NAEP questions dealing with multiculturalism. 4
NAEP questions dealing with any
basic principle of freedom. 0

Since 2002, federal funding of education to the states has been partially tied to the performance of students on the NAEP test. What issues will states emphasize if they want their students to do well— basic human rights such as life, liberty and ownership of private property—or environmentalism? Once again, the answer is obvious.

Basic information about the environment should be taught in our schools. The overemphasis of environmentalism, however, is undesirable. This overemphasis is obvious in the national tests and nationwide textbooks, and is, unfortunately, the order of the day.

RELIGIOUS ENVIRONMENTALISM

There are, today, two common approaches to protecting the environment. The first approach, that held by most Americans including the author, is the goal of being good stewards, or caretakers, of the environment. Our goal is to manage the environment so that it doesn't deteriorate but improves, instead. Key words in this approach are "stewards,""caretakers,""managers," and "conservation."

The second approach to protecting the environment is inherently religious. The goal of this approach is not to "manage" the environment, but to be "one with" the environment. This religious approach places human beings on the same level with animals, trees, and even rocks and lakes. It is often a pantheistic approach (everything is god) and/or an earth-worship approach of some kind. Key words in this approach are "being one with nature," being "brothers" and "sisters" with the animals or the trees, and respecting "Mother Earth" (with capital letters).

Most Americans are supportive of teaching the stewardship approach to the environment. Unfortunately, however, the religious view of environmentalism is predominant in the new Federal Curriculum. For example, the federal government's one achievement test, the NAEP, includes a number of questions based, in part, on the following narration (8th grade level test):

> ...there was once a Lakota holy man called Drinks Water, who dreamed what was to be; and this was long before the coming of the [whites]. He dreamed that the four-leggeds were going back into the earth and that a strange race had woven a spider's web all around the Lakotas. And he said: "When this happens, you shall live in square gray houses, in a barren land, and beside those gray houses you shall starve." They say he went back to Mother Earth soon after he saw this vision, and it was sorrow that killed him.

Since this wording is in the federal government's own test, the NAEP (which now serves as the model for all national achievement tests), it is especially significant. Notice the words, "he went back to

Mother Earth" (capital letters). This is the language of religious environmentalism. Another section of the NAEP test includes the following language:

> [Before the coming of the whites, people and animals] lived together like relatives....

This is, once again, the language of religious environmentalism, that of living in harmony with nature, not managing nature. A recent issue of *National Review* described the religious nature of contemporary environmentalism as it applies to the issue of drilling for oil on the North Slope of Alaska. *National Review* said:

> [The North Slope is] a religious icon, the Dome of the Rock of environmentalism. Indeed, among environmentalists, religious adjectives crowd out all others. [The North Slope] is "holy," "sacred," "divine," and "hallowed," [as stated] by the journalists and activists who just like knowing it's there. Drilling is therefore not just "greedy," but also sacrilegious. It would not matter, environmentalists insist, if there were a trillion barrels of oil safely extractable.... To them, drilling isn't bad policy, it's blasphemy.

Religious environmentalism is now standard fare in national textbooks. For example, the most recent Harcourt, Brace and Company series in language arts (1999 copyright) described our relationship with nature as follows (from the 4th grade reader in a story called "The People who Hugged the Trees"):

> Before she left the forest, Anrita kissed her special tree. Then she whispered, "Tree, if you are ever in trouble, I will protect you." The tree whispered back with a rustle of its leaves.... As Anrita grew, so did her love for the trees. Soon she had her own children, and she took them to the forest with her. "These [trees] are your brothers and sisters," she told them. [pp. T986 & T987]

One needn't look far to discover the kind of religious environmentalism that is evident in the reading selection above. The new tests and textbooks contain a steady diet of such writings. After all, *The National Standards for Civics and Government* said that the new standards were "useful in the development of...textbooks." [p. vi]

The new Federal Curriculum also said that the standards are "useful in the development of...curricular frameworks." [p. vi of the National Standards for Civics and Government] One such environmental curriculum has been developed in a Minnesota charter school and is called "Curriculum for Thematic Studies Grade Eleven." The school that developed this curriculum has been designated as a "model school" by the U.S. Department of Education.

The kind of environmentalism contained in this curriculum is not difficult to identify. Required activities, for example, include the following:

+ Discussion of aesthetic/spiritual values of water in *Walden*.
+ Read and analyze river myths from various cultures.
+ Postmodernism presentation.
+ *Spirit of Nature* video (Dalai Lama & Native American elder).
+ *Encounters with the Archdruid* discussions.
+ Field notes, journaling, meditations.

The resources listed for this particular curriculum on the environment include the following:

+ *Spirit in Nature* film clip with Dalai Lama.
+ Shaman and scientist.
+ "A Tibetan Buddhist Perspective on Spirit in Nature."
+ "Mother Earth: Nature as Living System."
+ *Hero with a Thousand Faces* by Joseph Campbell.
+ The Power of Myth by Joseph Campbell (excerpts and video clips).

The environmentalism being taught in this curriculum is obviously of a religious nature. The emphasis on the writing of Joseph Campbell is especially significant because Campbell is the most widely-read theologian of the New Age religion. New Age theology includes Pantheism and Earth worship within itself, often called Gaia theology.

The use of the term "Gaia" for Nature worship was popularized by James Lovelock, a NASA astrophysicist. Lovelock described Gaia this way:

> Gaia is Mother Earth. Gaia is immortal. She is the eternal source of life. She is surely a virgin. She does not need to reproduce herself as she is immortal. She is certainly the mother of us all, including Jesus.

In *The Power of Myth* referenced above, Joseph Campbell explained how to win converts to the New Age Religion. The way such converts are brought in, says Campbell, is this:

> Read myths. They teach you that you can turn inward, and you begin to get the message of the symbols. Read other people's myths, not those of your own religion, because you tend to interpret your own religion in terms of facts—but if you read the other ones, you begin to get the message.

Ever wonder why the new tests and textbooks include a steady diet of myths? Campbell says the reason for reading myths is that of getting people (students) involved in the New Age religion. Reading these myths also gets our students involved in religious environmentalism.

Religious environmentalism doesn't include just any religion, of course. Such environmentalism is adamantly opposed to Christianity because the Christian worldview sees human beings as being above nature and being the managers of nature, not as being "one with" nature. Religious environmentalism, in contrast, is the religion of paganism, spiritism and pantheism. Such religions see people, spirit and nature as one. For example, *Earth Ethics*, published by the Center for Respect of Life and the Environment, Fall 1998, says:

> The Temiar [a group living in the Malaysia rain forest] locate themselves...with the **interactive spirits of their**

environment.... In their dream they establish **kinship with spirits** who emerge, identify themselves, and give the gift of song. Receipt of a dream song from a **spiritguide** marks the pivotal moment in the development of **mediums** and healers. The song, sung during a ceremonial performance by the **medium** and an interactive female chorus, links **medium,** chorus, **trancedancers** and patient as they "follow the path" of the **spiritguide.** [Emphasis added.]

Descriptions of pagan theology and practice, like the one above, are commonplace throughout our educational and environmental materials, including school textbooks. Such materials make it crystal clear that the religion of environmentalism is now aggressively being taught to our children in the schools.

There is a close connection between the religion of environmentalism and the political agenda of many environmentalists. Tal Brooke comments on this connection when he says [in *One World*, End Run Publ., Berkeley, CA, 2000]:

[Gaia fits] handily into a centralized international order because it is collectivist and anti-individual as opposed to the Biblical view. It is also generically spiritual, and compulsively environmental, gathering up a broad variety of traditions. Gaia will boast of a broad-mindedness that includes Wiccans [witchcraft], neo-pagans, New Age groups, pagans, meditation groups, astrologers, gay and lesbian spirituality, and Eastern religions. It will be far less tolerant of Christian and conservative groups. [p. 64]

The internationalists correctly recognize that pagan earth religions are useful to their cause. They also recognize that Christianity presents a major roadblock to their political goals. For that reason, as the pagan religions are promoted, Christianity must be opposed. This is why we now commonly see a variety of subtle attacks on Christianity in the new education system. The following question from the 6th grade level Iowa Basics Test illustrates one of these attacks:

28. Which is the best evidence that the Roman Catholic Church was a powerful force in the Middle ages?
J. Many people were serfs.
K. Most European languages are based on Latin.
L. Most Christian leaders could read and write.
M. Large armies were persuaded to fight for the Holy Land.

The correct answer to this question is choice "M." thereby associating the actions of the Christian Church with the medieval wars known as the Crusades. Another case in point is contained in the reading section of this Iowa Basics exam. Six of those reading questions are based on a description of an Amish community in Ohio. The test's introduction to this reading selection reads as follows:

> Abe and Edna Miller and their four children operate a 150 acre farm in Ohio. They belong to a Christian group known as the Amish. Because of their religious beliefs, the Millers have no electricity or telephone. They farm with horses.

In this way, Christians are pictured as being isolated and primitive in how they run their lives. The Iowa Basics Test never says that the Amish are a sect, nor does it mention that the Amish are the exception, not the rule, insofar as Christian people are concerned.

Such distortions of Christianity are calculated and deliberate. The political agenda of the new education system includes undermining any sympathy toward Christianity that students may have as it indoctrinates them in the theology of environmentalism.

ENVIRONMENTALISM'S POLITICAL AGENDA

In the World Declaration on Education for All, 1990, the United States agreed to institute a national system of environmental education (under the supervision of UNESCO—the United Nations Education, Scientific, and Cultural Organization). That same year, PBS (the Public Broadcasting System) produced a video series on the environment called *After the Warming*.

In order to grasp the full impact of the political agenda of contemporary environmentalism, the author recommends that readers watch this video. The video calls for the creation of a Planetary Management Authority (PMA) which would have authority over the use of all the earth's resources.

Specifically, the Planetary Management Authority would do the following:

1. Create an international governmental agency that would have a higher level of authority than any of the nations of the earth.
2. Finance itself by establishing a PMA tax on all fossil fuels used in the world.
3. Require all countries to engage in mandatory family planning, as is now done in Communist China.
4. Outlaw the raising of beef cattle.
5. Double the cost of fossil fuels by means of the taxes it would impose or require.
6. Dictate how much carbon can be emitted into the atmosphere by every country of the world.
7. Create a world characterized by being "orderly." (Dictatorship is the most orderly form of government.)

Add up the specific characteristics of the PMA. It amounts to the creation of a one-world government. In this scenario, the nations would still exist, but they would be subservient to the new international government. The nations would become mere agencies for implementing the policies of the one-world government.

Does this sound far-fetched? Look at the facts: This video, and its overall plan, was created and published by the Public Broadcasting System (PBS) in consultation with various environmental groups. PBS is not a far-out radical group. This video contains the consensus of the environmental organizations involved. The overall plan of the environmental groups for one-world government is not the exception, it is the rule.

Perhaps it's time the American public knew what the ultimate goal of the environmentalists is all about.

CHAPTER TWELVE

Requiring Multiculturalism

What is wrong with this picture? The following list is contained in "CIVITAS: a Framework for Civic Education," published by the Center for Civic Education (CCE):

Fundamental Values of Freedom
1. The public good
2. Individual rights
3. Justice
4. Equality
5. Diversity
6. Truth
7. Patriotism

What is wrong with this picture? National sovereignty and natural law didn't make the list of "Fundamental Values of Freedom," but diversity did. Is diversity, also called "multiculturalism" and "tolerance," mentioned anywhere in the Declaration of Independence? Is diversity mentioned anywhere in the Constitution of the United States? Is diversity mentioned anywhere in the Federalist Papers? The fact of the matter is that diversity is never mentioned in any of these important documents which describe the "fundamental values" of our nation. Diversity, as the term is used today, is **not** a fundamental value of freedom in our nation, and it should **not** be included in this list.

If we were to construct an accurate list of the "fundamental values of freedom," as based on the Declaration of Independence (which describes the actual values of our nation), it would read as follows:

Fundamental Values of Freedom
1. National sovereignty
2. Natural law
3. Natural (God-given) and unalienable rights
   (a) The right to life
   (b) The right to liberty
   (c) The right to pursue happiness (private property)
4. Equality
5. Individual sovereignty (the voters hold the political power)

Even though diversity is absent from all of our nation's foundational documents, diversity is, nevertheless, not only present but is even emphasized in the new Federal Curriculum. Its emphasis is apparent from the following table:

Table 7
Number of Times Various Terms Are Included in the
National Standards on Civics and Government

References to the environment 17
References to natural law 1
References to the Second Amendment 0
References to national sovereignty 8
References to diversity 42

The following list makes obvious that, in the new Federal Curriculum, the teaching of multiculturalism (diversity) is far more important than teaching natural law, national sovereignty, or the right to bear arms.

THE POLITICAL IDEOLOGY OF MULTICULTURALISM

Since diversity is not an important value of freedom in the United States, why is it required (as a high priority) in the new Federal Curriculum? And what is multicultural education, anyway? The true nature of multicultural education was accurately described by New York Times book critic, Richard Bernstein, who said (*American Experiment Quarterly*, Summer, 1998):

> Multiculturalism is a code word for a left-wing political program. [p. 14]...When the diversity advocates talk about diversity, it is a code word for political ideology. [p. 17]

Once again, we see that the new Federal Curriculum is more concerned about the promotion of a political ideology/worldview than about teaching academic information. What is this worldview that is required in the Federal Curriculum? In the article referenced above, Bernstein also said:

> One of multiculturalism's main features is its denigration of the West [including the United States and including attacks against Christianity]. [p. 15]

An explicit example of Bernstein's description of multiculturalism was evident in a recent opinion piece written by William Jefferson Clinton. The former president first applauded diversity by saying:

> Fourth, from a political point of view, you might have said the dominant factor of the 21st-century world will be the explosion of diversity.... There was a breathtaking increase in ethnic, racial and religious diversity, proving that it's possible for people of different belief systems to live and work together. [Minneapolis *Star Tribune*, 1-13-02]

Former President Clinton followed up that glowing description of diversity by making the following statement:

Terror has been around a long time. The West has not always been blameless. In the First Crusade, when Christian soldiers seized Jerusalem, they burned a synagogue with 300 Jews and proceeded to slaughter every Muslim woman and child on the Temple Mount. My country is now the oldest continuous democracy in the world. Yet, it was born with legalized slavery, and many black slaves and Native Americans were terrorized and killed afterward. [Minneapolis *Star Tribune*, 1-13-02]

Clinton's statements may or may not be accurate, but that is not the point. The point is that Bill Clinton has been highly selective in choosing these particular examples. The purpose of the examples is obviously to denigrate the West in general, and the United States and Christianity in particular. No similar atrocities are cited which deal with any non-Western nations or that mention any non-Christian religions. This anti-West, anti-American, and anti-Christian perspective is standard fare in the value system known as multiculturalism. (William Clinton has been extraordinarily influential in shaping the new Federal Curriculum, of course.)

Another feature of multicultural education, as also suggested above, is that it is totally one-sided. Diversity education normally describes the supposedly exploited groups in glowing terms, while white, male, European, American or Christian individuals are pictured in a negative way. For example, the federal government's NAEP test portrays the American settlers as follows:

When I was older, I learned what the fighting was about. Upon the Madison Fork the Wasichus [white settlers] had found much of the yellow metal that they worship and that makes them crazy, and they wanted to have a road up through our country to the place where the yellow metal was....

Is that an accurate description of most white settlers—as people who "worship" gold which "makes them crazy"? In contrast to the negative view that we often find of white settlers, however, Native Americans are consistently pictured as peace-loving and noble. Negative details about Native Americans, such as the well-documented cannibalism practiced by Indians in the Southwest, are never mentioned.

If multicultural education were to be genuine, said Bernstein, it would include accurate and balanced information like the following:

> The truth of the matter is this: if you want real multiculturalism, get on an airplane and go someplace else—out there in that great region of the world called Abroad, where practices like female circumcision abound, along with amputation of the hands of thieves, head-to-foot veils for women, and death sentences for those who write supposedly "blasphemous" books. That place called Abroad, by the way, is not where tolerance for homosexuality was invented, or equal rights for women, or the phrase about all men being born equal and endowed by their creator with certain unalienable rights was struck. [p. 14, *American Experiment Quarterly*, Summer, 1998]

Multicultural education is a fraud. Time and attention that should be used to teach our children about our nation's history, geography, and government, is used, instead, to indoctrinate our children in a falsified, anti-American political ideology. In addition, the negative influence of multicultural education is carried over to the other academic disciplines. For example, reading selections in literature books are chosen, not because of their literary merit, but rather because the story, or its author, or both, represent one of the supposedly exploited classes. No wonder many children find school to be hopelessly dull.

In addition, new and trendy approaches to teaching mathematics are often based on the premise that some ethnic, racial, and gender groups learn mathematics in different ways than white males learn mathematics. What total nonsense.

As a consequence of multicultural education, both subject matter and teaching methods are now chosen because of their political correctness, not because of their academic value. And the children who are hurt the most are those who most desperately need quality, academic education—the minority members themselves.

Since multicultural education is harmful to our students, why is it a required learning area of the new Federal Curriculum? It is required because the new Federal Curriculum is more concerned about ideological agendas than about quality education. A textbook in college freshman orientation describes multiculturalism as follows (from *Orientation to College: A Reader*, by Elizabeth Steltenpohl et. al. Ed., Wadsworth Publ. C., Belmont, CA, 1996):

> In order to view multicultural education as an empowerment strategy, one must first take seriously the notion that **education can serve as an effective vehicle for social change.** [Emphasis added.]

Social change is the reason multicultural education is a required theme in the Federal Curriculum. The following section will describe how this works.

POSTMODERNIST IDEOLOGY

Multiculturalism carries with it the trendy new philosophy known as postmodernism. This ideological perspective was summarized by John Fonte, writing in *Policy Review*, January 2001, when he said:

> [The new Left teaches] that morals, values, truths, standards and human nature itself are products of different historical periods. There are no absolute moral standards that are universally true for all human beings outside of a particular historical context; rather morality [and truth] are "socially constructed."

The teaching of multiculturalism includes the teaching of postmodernism. Morality and truth become nothing more than cultural preferences that can, of course, be changed at any time. This is why postmodernists say there is nothing wrong with homosexual acts, permissive abortion, or any redefinitions of the family, such as choosing to become a single parent or legalizing homosexual marriage.

This radical ideology is also the reason the new system of education will not tolerate sex education programs that are abstinence-based.

There is a wealth of information which demonstrates that conventional sex education programs are a total failure and may even be counterproductive. There is also a wealth of information which demonstrates that abstinence-only sex education programs are extraordinarily successful. In spite of that information, the new education system insists on using the failed programs of the past. It refuses to use the effective programs. Why? The new Federal Curriculum is not about what works; it is all about indoctrinating our children with its ideology. When effectiveness clashes with ideology, as it usually does, ideology always wins.

The objective of teaching postmodernism to our children is accurately described in the following statement:

> We should teach students that knowledge is a **social construction**.... The classroom should become a forum in which multicultural debates concerning the construction of knowledge takes place. [Emphasis added, *Orientation to College: A Reader*, p. 176.]

This multicultural (and postmodernist) view that knowledge is a "social construct" (not genuine truth or reality) allows the political power-brokers to "reconstruct" history and truth to be anything they want it to be. Where does that take us? The bottom line for multicultural education, also as stated by *Orientation to College: A Reader*, is:

> This understanding [diversity] will enhance appreciation of the value and contributions of different cultures. It will also offer a vision of shared aspirations, respectful of diversity and differences, **on which a global society can be founded**. [Emphasis added, p. 113.]

Multiculturalism is a political agenda masquerading as an educational agenda. It consists—not of knowledge and appreciation of other cultures—but rather of the ideology that all cultures are equal, except for American culture, which is inferior. Multiculturalism also embraces postmodernism (knowledge is a mere social construct) and one-world government—since American culture and government is no better, and probably worse, than other cultures and government, we should all get together into one happy world family. (The most recent *Humanist Manifesto* also views multiculturalism as a building block of one-world government.)

THE RELIGIOUS CONTENT OF MULTICULTURAL EDUCATION

Multiculturalism not only has a clearly identifiable political agenda, it also has a religious agenda. The religious content of diversity was graphically described by World Net Daily (Jan. 11, 2002) as follows:

> BRAVE NEW SCHOOLS
> *Islam studies required in California district Course has 7th-graders memorizing Koran verses, praying to Allah*
> In the wake of Sept. 11, an increasing number of California public school students must attend an intensive three-week course on Islam, reports ASSIST News Service.
> The course mandates that 7th graders learn the tenets of Islam, study the important figures of the faith, wear a robe, adopt a Muslim name, and stage their own jihad....students must memorize many verses in the Koran, are taught to pray "in the name of Allah, the Compassionate, the Merciful" and are instructed to chant, "Praise to Allah, Lord of Creation."
> ...there are 25 Islamic terms that must be memorized, six Islamic (Arabic) phrases, 20 Islamic proverbs to learn along with Five Pillars of Faith and 10 key Islamic prophets and disciples to be studied....
> Nancy Castro, principal of Intermediate-Excelsior School of Byron, told ANS that the Islam course (included within "History of Culture") reflects California's educational standards....
> The textbook used for the Islamic course, *Across the Centuries*, is published by Houghton-Mifflin and has been adopted by the California school system. In it, according to ANS, Islam is presented broadly in a completely positive manner, whereas the limited references to Christianity are

"shown in a negative light, with events such as the Inquisition, and the Salem witch hunts highlighted in bold, black type."

The religious content of this class on culture (multiculturalism) is obvious. On the surface it may appear that the purpose of this class is to promote the Islamic religion. The purpose is that, but is also much broader than that. The primary reason for teaching Islam is to promote the view that all religions are equal—which is the central doctrine of the New Age religion. New Age guru, Joseph Campbell, says that the way to promote New Age theology is by teaching all religions. That way, says Campbell, students will learn the common themes of all religions, and these common themes form the center of New Age theology. Christianity, however, must be opposed because Christianity claims to have exclusive truth above and beyond what other religions recognize.

As stated in Chapter 11, New Age religion is also an integral part of modern day environmentalism. New Age theology is additionally an essential focus of the one-world government, the reason being that the "one-worlders" want to establish a common, non-Christian, one with the Earth, single-culture religion for the entire globe.

We may be appalled at the nature of the new Federal Curriculum, but one has to admit that it is remarkably consistent. Every theme is intertwined with every other theme, the result being a comprehensive worldview that is quite complete in its philosophy, ethics, politics, and religion. The worldview of the new Federal Curriculum is no small matter. This is the worldview which is in direct competition to the worldview that created the free country we know as the United States of America. The big battle of our time is the battle of ideas.

CHAPTER THIRTEEN

Restructuring Government

As was noted earlier, Shirley McCune, made the following statement in her article "Restructuring Education":

> Our society has undergone profound economic, demographic, and social transformation—a transformation that impacts virtually every aspect of our individual and collective lives. It is the manifestation of a new era of civilization...and the movement from a national to a global society. Virtually every institution is forced to restructure to meet a changed environment and changed needs. [*http://www.net/-building/ crfut_mccune.html*]

This statement by McCune is an accurate description of the thinking behind the new Federal Curriculum. The planners of the new system believe that we are becoming a brave new world, and they intend to help usher in this new world by transforming America so that we become part of a "global society." How does one restructure

America? One does so by restructuring our education program—and by restructuring all of government.

In order to fulfill their dream of restructuring America, the education planners must restructure government. That is why the *National Standards for Civics and Government* form the heart and center of the new Federal Curriculum. Changing our education system is the means to the end, not the end itself. In order to restructure America, the ultimate goal must be to restructure government.

RESTRUCTURING GOVERNMENT BY CENTRAL-PLANNING

Central-planning, as opposed to local decision-making, is a top-down approach to management. Central-planning systems make decisions in a manner that is far removed from the place and people where those decisions are implemented.

The new Federal Curriculum is a central-planning system. The most important policy decisions in education are being made by the federal government. States and local schools have been reduced to being mere agents of the federal government. Companies that write textbooks and national tests have not fared much better.

The central-planning approach to education is evident in the federally determined job skills known as SCANS (Secretary's Commission on Achieving Necessary Skills). Constructed by the federal government's Department of Labor in 1992, SCANS is a mammoth document which presumes to specify what job skills any worker needs for almost any occupation. In the past, it was the schools themselves, in conversations with employers and institutions of higher learning, that decided what job skills their graduates needed to have. Those job skills are now determined by, and dictated by, the federal government. (The federal laws passed in 1994, Goals 2000 and STW, stated that their requirements were largely based on SCANS.)

The folly of having job skills defined by the federal government by means of a central-planning system is evident from the following SCANS job skills—in this instance for the occupation of farming:

Participates as a Member of a Team (C09)
Handle manure (e.g. cleaning the barn and spreading the manure on the fields). To perform this task, one farmer

sets the spreader in place (farm hand A). The other farmer, using a tractor with a loader, fills the spreader (farm hand B). Then the first farmer spreads the manure on the field. Once manure is spread, both farmers use hand scrapers and shovels to clean areas missed by the tractor. **Task ID # 8091631**

In our country, no farmers operate this way. No free enterprise system will have one employee sitting in a tractor, waiting, while another employee fills the spreader. In our country, the same person is both farm hand A and farm hand B. One farmer (probably the owner) will get out of one tractor, go to the second tractor with the loader, and fill the spreader himself.

Notice that in this SCANS skill, teamwork is more important than efficiency. No farm in our country would stay in business if it valued teamwork more than efficiency. A second SCANS skill for farming reads as follows:

Responsibility (F13)
<u>Takes responsibility for accomplishing work assignments.</u>
To perform this task, the farmer ensures that work assignments are accomplished correctly and on time, such as ensuring that the cattle count is correct. **Task ID # 7131631**

Once again, farms in our nation do not function this way. In our nation, cattle are normally enclosed. There is no reason to count them. A farmer may look over the cattle to see if any appear to be sick, but counting the cattle is a waste of time. Notice that the SCANS skill above would not only have the cattle counted once, but twice, both by a low level employee and the supervisor. This is typical government bureaucracy as opposed to free enterprise. The example also illustrates why the central-planning system of socialism doesn't work.

A third SCANS skill for farming is stated as follows:

Responsibility (F13)
<u>Milk cows.</u> To perform this task, the farmer brings cows into the barn early in the morning and sets up the milking

equipment, and ensures proper operation. The farmer then brings the first cows into the milking parlor and feeds them by attaching milkers. The cows are treated medically, as necessary. **Task ID # 7131631**

The reader may wonder if this skill description is a misprint—it's not. The composers of this SCANS skill apparently don't realize that one end of the cow gets fed and the other end gives milk! Such is the nature of central-planning at the hands of government bureaucrats. Perhaps it would be better to have those actually involved in various jobs make the determination of what the required skills for those jobs should be.

How ironic it is that as Communist China is moving away from central-planning toward more local decision-making (one of the main reasons for China's rapid economic growth), the schools in our nation are being forced by the federal government to move in the opposite direction. Why, then, should America adopt central-planning systems that are known to be counterproductive?

There are two reasons: The first is a general anti-American sentiment that permeates the new education system. The SCANS report, for example, makes numerous negative comments about the United States and alleges that our education and economic systems are ill-equipped to meet the challenges of the 21st Century. In direct contrast, the SCANS report speaks of the Japanese economic system in glowing terms, referring to it with words like the "economic miracle" of the 20th Century.

Does Japan really have a better economic and educational system than the United States? The objective facts are these: Since SCANS was written (1992), the Japanese stock market has lost 75% of its value. Real estate in Japan has lost 80% of its value. In comparison to the dollar, the Japanese yen has lost 1/3 of its buying power. Why do investors buy dollars instead of yen? The reason is because the American economic system is considered by the world's business interests to be far stronger than the Japanese economy. Copying Japan makes no economic or educational sense, but that is what the new federal education system is doing. In spite of such facts, the SCANS report makes following admonitions:

The nation's school systems should make the SCANS foundation skills and workplace competencies explicit objectives of instruction at all levels. [p. 20 of the report] All employers, public and private, should incorporate the SCANS know-how into all their human resource development efforts. [p. 21]

A variety of federal laws, in particular Goals 2000, School-to-Work, and the Workforce Investment ACT (WIA), are now forcing the schools to incorporate SCANS into the school curriculum. This is central-planning at its worst.

Why is this happening? Why is a failed central-planning agenda being forced upon our schools? The second reason, and the primary reason, is stated in the SCANS report, itself, which says:

A student who accomplishes enough to meet an overall standard would be awarded a certificate of initial mastery (CIM), a **universally recognized statement** of experience and accomplishment. [Emphasis added, p. XiX.]

In this statement we see what SCANS is all about. The reason for SCANS is not that of having high standards, nor of having standards that fit actual employment needs. The reason for SCANS lies in the goal of having "universally recognized" (meaning, internationally recognized) standards for employment. SCANS is part of an international effort to specify job skills (with international skills certificates) for all jobs throughout the world.

A similar example was provided by Education Direct, a national jobs certification program, early in 2002 when it sent out a memo which said (*http://www.detc.org/*):

You can train with confidence knowing your program is accredited by the Distance Education and Training Council (DETC) which is listed by the U.S. Department of Education as a nationally recognized accrediting agency.

Sounds like national certification, doesn't it? It's really much more than that. Education Direct, on its website, states (*www.EduDirect-usa.com*):

Education Direct has been reviewed and approved as an Authorized Provider of continuing education and training programs by the **International** Association for Continuing Education and Training (IACET). [Emphasis added.]

Federal job skills are much more than nationally defined skills; they are internationally defined job skills. That is why SCANS has to be a central-planning system. If the determination of useful job skills were left up to local schools and local business, they would not be designed for some job in Germany or Japan. Even though central-planning is always a disaster, nevertheless, the utopian dream of having a one-world economy—without borders and where all workers are trained the same way—takes precedence over economic growth, productivity, and freedom.

SCANS is not the only central-planning portion of the new Federal Curriculum. Goals 2000, School-to Work, and the Workforce Investment Act (passed in 1998) all consist of federal guidelines that states are forced to accept. The states are required to submit plans to the federal government, and federal bureaucrats then determine if the state plans conform to the federal guidelines. If the plans do not conform, the states are required to revise their plans until the federal regulations are satisfied. This is a central-planning system from start to finish.

The reason for this central-planning in all the relevant federal laws is the same as the reason for central-planning in SCANS. As was mentioned in Chapter 7, the World Declaration for Education for All (1990) clarified that the countries which signed on have all agreed to teach the same themes that the Federal Curriculum is now forcing upon all American schools. The significance of these international standards was underscored in the New Standards Project (led by Marc Tucker and Lauren Resnick) which said:

It is critical in our view, that, whatever national examination system is established, it reflect **international Standards** of performance. It is very unlikely that will happen if all fifty states and the territories have to agree on the standard. [Emphasis added.]

That is, we are not just dealing with a Federal Curriculum, we are really dealing with an International Curriculum. The two are the same. The grand idea is to require the same values, the same knowledge, and the same job skills, to produce a unified world culture and a single, unified world economy.

In a speech called "Viewed from Afar: A New Meaning for World-Class Standards in Education," presented at CIVITAS@PRAGUE, 1995, R. Freeman Butts described the new education system as follows (R. Freeman Butts is the Senior Consultant for the CCE):

> Comenius antedated our contemporary calls for world-class standards by proposing an outlook called pan-sophism, i.e., **teaching a common body of universal knowledge to all children everywhere** that could pave the road to universal peace in a war-torn world. He envisioned a **universal system of schools** in which the whole human race could be educated, including all ages, [lifelong learning] all social classes, both sexes, and all nations: a truly **universal education (panpaedia)**... This effort could be a giant step forward in **redefining "world class standards"** in education.... [Emphasis added.]

The new education system frequently uses the term "world class standards." Many people do not know what that term means. The quotation above defines the term accurately.

One-world curriculum, one-world values, one-world culture, one-world job skills, one-world economy, universal system of schools—that is what the new Federal Curriculum is all about. Such utopian dreams require massive central-planning. That is why workability is replaced with central-planning. A one-world system cannot be put into place without it.

EVADING THE TENTH AMENDMENT

As Hillary Clifton's close friend, Marc Tucker, pointed out, a system of federal standards would never be adopted by the states if they were allowed to govern their own education systems. Federal control of education would be a necessity. There was, of course, one big problem—the Tenth Amendment to the United States Constitution. This amendment reads as follows:

> *The powers not delegated to the United States by the Constitution, nor prohibited by it to the States, are reserved to the States respectively, or to the people.*

This amendment marks the last, and culminating, amendment in the Bill of Rights. The amendment clarifies that the people and the states retain all rights not specifically given to the federal government by the Constitution. This is why the Tenth Amendment has often been regarded as the most important amendment in the Bill of Rights. The amendment clarified that ultimately all rights reside with the people, and that the federal government had only those rights delegated to it by the Constitution. For that reason, the rights of the federal government are called "delegated rights." All other rights are "reserved rights," rights reserved to the states and the people. Historically, the setting of education policy has been regarded as one of the reserved rights.

How did the new federal education system manage to evade the Tenth Amendment? It happened like this: The 1994 laws that put the federal government in charge of education policy in our nation—those laws being Goals 2000 and School-to-Work—were laws that repeatedly said the new system was "voluntary." Who could complain if the new program was voluntary? Why should the courts object to voluntary standards? Who could dissent if the states could participate if they wanted to and could refuse to sign on if they so desired?

This language of the programs which said they were "voluntary" was also part of a massive propaganda campaign. Most Senators and Representatives were totally fooled. Many even defended their vote in support of these terrible bills on the grounds that the new programs were supposedly voluntary.

Most elected officials didn't realize (the architects of the bills knew, of course) that the 1994 bill which funded all other federal education programs, HR6, stipulated that the U.S. Department of Education could withhold all federal education money from any state that didn't comply with Goals 2000 and STW. That is why the states all signed on, even though a few tried to hold out for a while. Since federal funding amounts to about 9% of all funding for K-12 education, the states held their noses and said yes to the federal agenda.

Is this a violation of the Tenth Amendment? It certainly is. But then, the education dreamers intend to rewrite the Constitution, not honor it. (The example above also demonstrates that the new Federal Curriculum has been constructed to deliberately mislead both elected officials and the American public. The bills continually said "voluntary," when the entire structure made them far more mandatory than voluntary. This kind of deception occurs throughout the Federal Curriculum.)

RESTRUCTURING AMERICA FOR
INTERNATIONAL GOVERNANCE

We know how the architects of our nation viewed national sovereignty (see Chapter 8). They began and ended the Declaration of Independence with this principle. They made it clear that national sovereignty is the most fundamental principle of freedom in the United States of America. If this principle is to be maintained, then the authority of the United States must be greater than the authority of any international organizations. It is important, then, that national sovereignty be honestly taught in our schools. Such will be the case if America's history and the Declaration of Independence are merely presented in an accurate manner.

If the new Federal Curriculum were true to the fundamental principles of the United States, it would include statements stressing the importance of national sovereignty. Does the Federal Curriculum make such statements? No. Instead, we find statements like the following (*National Standards for Civics and Government*, p. 126):

> **United States and international organizations.** *Students should be able to evaluate, take, and defend positions about what the relationship of the United States should be to international organizations.*

Notice that the standards do not say that the United States is sovereign; nor do they say that this sovereignty should be maintained. Does the quotation above then mean that the Federal Curriculum has no position on this all-important question? Not at all (see Chapter 8.) It only means that, for political reasons, the Curriculum must be a bit indirect in its phraseology.

What, then, is the position of the Federal Standards on the question of national sovereignty? HR6, the 1994 education funding law, authorized and funded the CCE to write the Federal Curriculum in the form of a textbook called "We the People: The Citizen and the Constitution." This textbook says:

> ...the issues confronting American citizens are increasingly **international** [textbook's emphasis]. Issues of economic competition, the environment, and the movement of peoples around the world require an awareness of **political associations that are larger than the nation state.** [Emphasis added, p. 202.]

What is meant by "an awareness of political associations larger than the nation state"? *We the People* continues by saying:

> The culture we live in is becoming **cosmopolitan,** [textbook's emphasis] that is, belonging to the whole world. [p. 202]

Creating a common world culture is one of the primary objectives of the new Federal Curriculum. For what reason? *We the People: The Citizen and the Constitution* explains as follows:

> National corporations have become international.... Environmental concerns transcend national boundaries. Entertainment—music, sports and film—command worldwide markets.... The achievements of modern technology are turning the world into a **global village** [one-world government] with shared cultural, economic, and environmental concerns. [Textbook's emphasis, p. 202.]

Keep in mind that *We the People* is a model curriculum for government. What, then, are the implications of the statements above? If we fill in the blanks in the analogies, the implications are as follows:

+ Just as national corporations have become international—government must also become international.
+ Just as environmental concerns transcend national boundaries—government must also transcend national boundaries.
+ Just as culture has become cosmopolitan (belonging to the whole world)—government must also become cosmopolitan (belonging to the whole world.)

What is this "global village" that is being advocated by this textbook? The section of the book quoted above ends with this question for all our students: "Do you think that world citizenship will be possible in your lifetime?" There can't be world citizenship without a sovereign world government, of course. That is what "global village" means.

The 1994 law instructed the Center for Civic Education to write standards to educate students "about the history and principles of the Unites States." How ironic it is, then, that those standards actually undermine the "principles of the United States" and instead advocate one-world government. Maybe it's time that Congress and the American public learned the truth about these standards.

What will a one-world government be like? The new book by Professor Michael Hardt and Antonio Negro, called *Empire*, describes this brave new world in detail. (*Time* Magazine approvingly called this book, "the hot, smart book of the moment." It was also on the Amazon.com top-100 best-seller list, and it made the New York University's top 10 list.)

Empire's purpose, say the authors, is to describe "the world to come." It will be a world, they say, where nations cease to exist as sovereign states because they have been rendered impotent by the all-powerful world government. This new world order, say the authors, will eliminate all private property, rule with an iron fisted international police force, and will have total control of all communications—print media, radio and TV and, yes, especially the internet. In this brave new world, the authors say, freedom will be a relic of the past, justice will be redefined to mean whatever the police force is able to do, and society will be described as "the society of control."

Why, then, will the citizens of the United States, and why will other citizens of the free world, be willing to give up their freedom to be ruled by a total dictatorship run by a police force? They will do so, say the authors, because those who run this new dictatorship will "directly organize the brains" of the people of the world so that we all comply with whatever the new social planners want us to do. This "social engineering" the authors say, will be so complete that:

> Society, subsumed with a power that reaches down to the ganglia of the social structure and its process of develop-ment, reacts like a single body. Power is thus expressed as a control that extends throughout the depths of the con-sciousness and bodies of the population....[p. 24]

That is, all communication, including the media and education, will be used to control the population of the world. Sound farfetched? Think about it. It is difficult to imagine that a one-world government could function any other way.

CHAPTER FOURTEEN

Redefining Education as Job Skills

This chapter will deal with the question: Should our nation continue to educate its citizens beyond their vocational station in life? Traditionally our education system has said "yes" to that question. One of the reasons for saying yes is this—how can we know what a person's vocational station in life is until they have had the opportunity to explore a variety of different options? The new Federal Curriculum sees it differently. The new Federal Curriculum holds that no one should be educated beyond his or her vocational station in life.

For example, the School-to-Work portion of the new Federal Curriculum often presents the following facts to promote its agenda. These facts, usually printed in large letters, are:

- 180,000 Truck Drivers have Baccalaureate Degrees.
- 270,000 Sales People have Baccalaureate Degrees.

Most Americans, when confronted with these facts, probably shrug their shoulders and say, "So What"? Most of us think that it is good for people to be well educated regardless of the occupation they hold at any particular time. The new Federal Curriculum, in contrast, sees these same facts in a negative light. The new system believes that society has wasted its resources on anyone who is a truck driver or a salesclerk and who also has a college degree.

Following this line of thinking, the new education system frequently refers to students as being "human resources." Resources for what? The new Federal Curriculum views our children as being human resources for large corporations. (Just as businesses need electricity, steel, glass, plastics, and the like to make their products, they also need human resources.) Students are also referred to as "human capital"—just like money in the bank or like other raw materials that are used to manufacture some product and to make a profit for the company.

It is true, of course, that students are human resources. Is that all they are? Don't human beings have value above and beyond being resources for business? If they do, shouldn't people be well educated regardless of whether they happen to need every last subject for their vocation?

This is why the new Federal Curriculum wants students to have a career pathway by the time they are in 8th grade. (The federal government has assigned various "career clusters" to each of the fifty states as part of the central-planning mentality of the new system. Minnesota, for example, has been assigned mining of minerals as one of its career clusters—even though the mining industry in Minnesota is basically dead.)

By requiring 8th graders to have careers, society avoids "wasting resources" on their training. The idea is that someone going into truck driving or sales-clerking doesn't need much math, biology or literature, so he or she won't study that much of it.

Our children are now being viewed the same way we view the stock market—any investment should produce a profit, and if it won't produce a profit, the investment won't be made. That is, our children are not to learn anything that will not make them a more valuable resource to business.

This new system raises important questions, the main one being: Who should be the primary beneficiary of our education system? Traditionally, America's education program has existed for the best interests of the child. Not any more. The new Federal Curriculum reflects the belief that education now exists for the best interests of big business.

Once we determine who the beneficiary of our education program is, it is then relatively easy to design an effective method to meet the needs of our client. Why, then, has our education system been changed from one which included broad-based academic knowledge with numerous opportunities, to one that is now strictly vocational? The reason the program has changed is because the client has changed. Education no longer serves the child, it now serves corporations.

In the past we believed that if students obtained a broad base of knowledge (general education), they would then be prepared to enter a wide range of different careers. They would be equipped to make wise decisions about which career is best for them. They would have the necessary background to change careers when needed. In addition, they would be equipped to be good parents, good spouses, good citizens, and good employers and employees.

Ironically, when all education becomes vocational, the quality of employees that such education produces will actually deteriorate, not improve. We can expect that the global competitiveness of our nation will decline as well. To illustrate this truth, let us ask the question: What nation, over the past fifty years, has led the world in high technology and other innovations? Has it been Japan? Has it been Germany? How about England? The answer is none of these. The country that has been the world leader in technology and innovations of all kinds has been the United States.

Why has that been? There are two reasons. In the first place, we have had an economic system that has been free, and, for that reason, has encouraged innovations. Secondly, we have had an education system that has provided students with a broad background of knowledge that has equipped them to be innovative as well. Vocationalizing education can give us workers; it will not give us innovators. (Existing businesses may not want innovations, of course. They may prefer, instead, to protect their own turf and to discourage competition.)

We will not be the first country to reduce education to mere job training. Consider the following quotation:

> Every bit of knowledge one acquires should be accompanied by a demonstration of how it can be applied to the practical needs of society.
>
> —Vladimir Lenin

What is the difference in meaning between Lenin's statement above and the statement below from the new Federal Curriculum?

> This workshop will outline a strategy for integrating academic and vocational courses around career majors.
> —2000 School-to-Work Conference, Minneapolis, MN

The meaning of the two statements is the same. Both statements mean that all education is vocational. This is not to say that the new American system of education is a communist system. It's an international system of universally defined job skills (see Chapter 12). It is also a totalitarian system, and totalitarian systems do not like well-educated people.

This concludes the description of the content of the new Federal Curriculum. Once again, that content is:

1. Undermining national sovereignty.
2. Redefining natural rights.
3. Minimizing natural law.
4. Promoting environmentalism.
5. Requiring multiculturalism.
6. Restructuring government.
7. Redefining education as job skills.

We now turn to the enforcement of this new curriculum.

PART III

Enforcing the New Federal Curriculum

CHAPTER FIFTEEN

Indoctrination,
Not Education

How is the new Federal Curriculum being imposed upon our schools? There are numerous ways. This chapter will provide a case study of one of the many techniques now being used to force the new curriculum into the schools.

We observed in Chapter 8 that the new Federal Curriculum requires a weakening of the natural rights, those rights called "unalienable" by the Declaration of Independence. This chapter will reveal one way that the Federal Curriculum weakens these natural rights and instead promotes the international view of human rights.

The example comes from the high school textbook in civics and government called *We the People: The Citizen and the Constitution*. This is the textbook that was authorized and funded by the federal law known as HR6 (1994). The textbook was written to provide the new Federal Standards in civics and government to all schools in textbook form. For that reason, any school can comply with the new standards by simply using this textbook. The book was written by the Center for Civic Education (CCE). On page 208, the textbook says (the complete text of the Universal Declaration of Human Rights is included in the Appendixes of this book):

Critical Thinking Exercise
**EXAMINING THE UNIVERSAL
DECLARATION OF HUMAN RIGHTS [1948]**
Review the Universal Declaration of Human Rights found in the Reference Section and answer the following questions:
1. What rights does the Universal Declaration of Human Rights proclaim that are not in the U.S. Constitution and Bill of Rights?
2. What rights in our Constitution and Bill of Rights are not included in the Universal Declaration of Human rights? Why, do you suppose they are not included?
3. What appears to be the purpose of the rights in the Universal Declaration of Human Rights that are not protected by our Constitution or Bill of Rights?
4. Examine each of the rights in the Universal Declaration of Human Rights that is not protected specifically in our Constitution. Is the right you have identified protected in the United States by other means, such as civil rights legislation; civil or criminal law contracts between private parties; labor and management agreements on unemployment benefits, vacation pay, and sick leave; custom or tradition; other means not listed above?
5. What rights, if any, in the Universal Declaration of Human Rights should be established in the United States? How should they be established? Explain your position.
6. How do the rights listed in the Universal Declaration of Human Rights appear to reflect the history and experiences of the time in which it was written?

Numerous objections could be made about the nature of this supposed "critical thinking" assignment for high school students. Suffice it to say that the study questions do not put the Universal Declaration of Human Rights in the negative light that it deserves. On the contrary, after the exercise it could be expected that most students would view the Universal Declaration of Human Right in a positive way. Indeed, the exercise has been structured to lead the student to believe that the Universal Declaration of Human Rights is as good as, or superior to, the Bill of Rights of the U.S. Constitution.

This assignment reminds one of the way that magicians perform tricks. Magicians draw the attention of the audience away from the location where the real action is taking place. The mechanics of the trick then occur someplace where the audience is not looking at that particular time. This assignment works the same way. The textbook questions focus the student's attention to superficial differences between our Bill of Rights and the Universal Declaration of Human Rights. The student's attention is drawn away from the important difference, not toward it. As a consequence, the student is given an incorrect understanding of the important difference between the U.S. Bill of Rights and the Universal Declaration of Human Rights.

The important difference is this: The American Bill of Rights was based upon the framework of the Declaration of Independence which states that the primary purpose of government is to protect the natural rights. The Declaration says, "that to secure these rights, Governments are instituted among Men." That is, human rights must come first, other interests of government must come second. Stated simply, human rights trump other government interests. The natural human rights have higher priority than other governmental values.

In direct contrast to the American view of human rights, The Universal Declaration of Human Rights states (Article 29, paragraph 3): "These rights and freedoms may in no case be exercised contrary to the purposes and principles of the United Nations."

In the Universal Declaration of Human Rights, then, which has the higher authority—human rights or the United Nations? According to the Universal Declaration, the United Nations has the higher authority. Stated simply, the interests of the United Nation trump the basic human rights.

Looked at superficially, however, the Universal Declaration of Human Rights may not seem to be all that much different from our Bill of Rights. As soon as we understand what these statements mean, however, we can then see that the two documents are actually direct opposites. In our system of government, the rights of every person are the highest authority. In the Universal Declaration of Human Rights, the UN as a governing body is the highest authority.

The significance of this difference would be difficult to overstate. The view of the American Bill of Rights is the view of freedom. The view of the Universal Declaration is the view of tyranny.

Compare the two fundamental views of human rights to the following descriptions of human rights (as correctly stated by Margaret Stimman Branson in her article called, "Rights: an International Perspective," Marina del Rey, CA, June 21, 1991):

> "Citizens of the USSR have the right to work and the right to choose their trade in accordance with...the needs of society [as determined by the government]." [Article 41 of the Constitution of the former Soviet Union]

> "The exercise by citizens...of their freedoms and rights may not infringe upon the interests of the state." [Article 51 of the Chinese Constitution]

> "Citizens have freedom of speech in keeping with the goals of the socialist society." [Constitution of Cuba, Article 52]

As can be seen, the view of human rights contained in the Universal Declaration of Human Rights is exactly the same as the view in the communist constitutions quoted above. In communist governments, government interests come first, human rights come second. When human rights come second, they mean nothing at all.

Remember that Stimmann Branson said that the Universal Declaration on Human Rights was an attempt to "combine the competing conceptions" of human rights. That type of synthesis is like mixing oil and water. In that mix, tyranny will always rise to the top.

The conclusion of the matter is this: The new Federal Curriculum, as it deals with the Universal Declaration of Human Rights, misleads students into thinking that this international statement of human rights is an acceptable statement, on a par with the U.S. Bill of Rights. The exact opposite is true, however. Under the guise of a "critical thinking exercise," the Federally funded and sanctioned textbook is engaging in propaganda, not education. The purpose of the propaganda is to undermine the basic principles of our nation and to replace them with the principles of one-world government. Such is the nature of the new Federal Curriculum.

CHAPTER SIXTEEN

Taking Over
Baby Education

The new education system is extraordinarily interested in imposing the new Federal Curriculum on early childhood education—also known as "baby ed" and as "birth-to-kindergarten" education. The backers of the new radical system recognize that a person's most fundamental attitudes and values are heavily influenced, if not formed, during the first five years of life. For that reason, the planners and advocates of the new system of education are now imposing the new Federal Curriculum into this early childhood education process.

The high level of interest in the education of our children from birth to kindergarten is evident in the World Declaration on Education for All, 1990, which states:

> *Learning begins at birth.* This calls for early childhood care and initial education. These can be provided through arrangements involving families, communities, or institutional programmes, as appropriate. [Article V]

Notice that the World Declaration does not say that early child-hood education can be actually provided by families. On the contrary, it says that early childhood education can be provided by "arrangements involving families." The World Declaration intends to institute governmental control of the world's preschool children. This govern-mental control means that someone other than parents or grandpar-ents will educate their children from birth on up. The World Declaration on Education for All also calls for:

Expansion of early childhood care and developmental activities, including family and community interventions.... [Goals and Targets section of the "Action Plan" of the World Declaration on Education for All]

The "developmental activities" for early childhood refers, once again, to baby education. Notice that "expansion of early childhood" education is not limited to "disadvantaged" children; it is intended for all children. The World Declaration on Education for All also states:

The preconditions for educational quality, equity and effi-ciency, **are set in the early childhood years**, making atten-tion to early childhood care and development essential to the achievement of basic education goals. [Emphasis added, section I., 3.]

Translated this means that the basic attitudes and values of the child are largely determined in the first five years of life. For that reason, the international planners must take over the care of these youngest of children. The statement above also says that doing so is "essential to the achievement of basic education goals." What are these "basic education" goals? The World Declaration on Education for All defines these goals as follows:

...to achieve **environmental protection** [see Chapter 11 of this book], to be **tolerant** towards social and religious sys-tems which differ from their own [see Chapter 12 of this book], accepted **humanistic values and human rights** are upheld [as defined by the Universal Declaration of Human Rights, Appendix B] and to work for **international** peace and **solidarity** in an interdependent world [one-world government]. [Emphasis added, Article I of the Action Plan.]

As can be seen above, the stated goals of the World Declaration on Education for All are essentially the same as the themes of the new Federal Curriculum. Should we be surprised? This means that, according to the World Declaration, the goal of baby education is to indoctrinate our youngest children with the attitudes, values and worldview contained in the new Federal Curriculum.

It works like this: The first goal of the Goals 2000 law states that "By the year 2000, all children will start school ready to learn." The federal government's 2002 education funding bill, in turn, clarified how this education of preschool children will be carried out. This 2002 funding bill, while describing early childhood education, stipulated that the U.S. Secretary of Education shall require "other measures of program impact as the Secretary determines to be appropriate." (Sec. 2151 A. iii.)

What are these requirements which the Secretary of Education determines to be appropriate for early childhood education? The requirements include the NAEYC standards (National Association for the Education of Young Children). These standards are already required for all Head Start programs with 20 or more children. The intention of the new education system, however, is to require these standards for all nonparental childcare from birth to kindergarten. Seven states already require NAEYC certification for all state-funded pre-kindergarten programs.

What are these NAEYC requirements for the caregivers of young children and preschool teachers? They include the same anti-academic indoctrination that makes up the new Federal Curriculum. Acceptable caregivers are described by the NAEYC standards as follows:

> Mathematics instruction should be guided by the...standards developed by the NCTM [National Council for Teaching Mathematics].... According to NCTM understanding [of math] develops through interaction

with...[and] in settings where students have opportunities to **construct their own relationships** when they first meet a new topic. [Emphasis added.]

That is, even mathematical knowledge is viewed as a "construct" (invention of a culture), not as something that is factual or true. Acceptable caregivers are also described as follows:

They know the sociopolitical contexts of major language groups and how this may affect a child's motivation to learn English. They know the benefits of bilingualism....

It doesn't matter to the new Federal Curriculum that bilingual education has proven to be disastrous for minority children, as the repeal of bilingual education in California has demonstrated. The new education system is not interested in the academic success for the children of minorities. The new system is more concerned about promoting the Marxist and one-world political philosophy than in having all our children succeed.

Not surprisingly, the radical new civics curriculum is also specifically included in the NAEYC standards. The NAEYC description of caregivers states:

Social Relations / Civics: Become a participating member of the group giving up some individuality for the greater good.

As was noted in Chapter 9, this de-emphasis of individuality and the corresponding emphasis on the "greater good" of society is one of the primary building blocks of one-world government. Our most vulnerable children will now be indoctrinated with this ethic of one-world control.

Another feature of the NAEYC system is what it calls the "anti-bias" standards. This anti-bias value-system is described by NAEYC as follows:

...in order to make curriculum powerful and accessible to all, well prepared candidates develop curriculum that is free of biases related to ethnicity, religion, gender, or ability status....[Meaning that multicultural education is required—see Chapter 12 of this book.]

What does a curriculum "free of biases" look like? NAEYC illustrates the curriculum to the children's caregivers in the form of a book called *A Teacher's Guide to Activism with Young Children*. As the title suggests, this teacher's guide instructs teachers on how to turn birth-to-kindergarten children into political activists! (Sounds like something we would expect from hard-core communists.) Specifically, this *Teacher's Guide* tells teachers how to make their preschool children into activists on the following issues:

1. Environmentalism.
2. Multiculturalism, including acceptance of homosexuality.
3. Opposition to the military and to military armaments.

Why should caregivers be teaching political activism to preschool children? The answer, according to the NAEYC approved text called *That's Not Fair: A Guide to Activism in Young Children*, is because "Anti-bias activism has other intrinsic benefits for young children." These benefits, according to the text, "provide a mental model for children at risk from bias" and "provide a model for equity and justice for privileged dominant culture children." In this way, children from minorities are encouraged to worry about the possibility of bias while majority member children are taught to feel guilty about their position in life, a fact of life over which they have no control.

Behind this anti-bias curriculum lies the Marxist dogma that emphasizes the division between the supposed exploiting class of people and the supposed exploited class. This discredited worldview, which always places one group of people in opposition to another, is central to the "anti-bias" curriculum.

This Marxist paradigm is typically applied to the gay rights agenda. The following section from the *Teacher's Guide to Activism with Young Children* provides the following model for teaching gay rights to our youngest children:

Each year she reads [before nap each day] *The Trumpet of the Swan*...[to teach activism].... The second part of the book focuses on the swan's courtship and mating. When Ann reads the book, she changes the gender of the main character from a male to a female swan. When the main character becomes female, her courtship of another female swan becomes the story of two women falling in love. This invariably provokes conversation among the children about women marrying women and men marrying men. It's important to Ann that children feel comfortable with people who are lesbian and gay and to feel relaxed and at ease with them. When Ann reads this book, the kids care deeply about Louise the swan by the time she begins to court Serena, her true love. They can't easily dismiss or ignore her, because they are invested in her love and happiness. So the classroom conversations about Louise marrying Serena are grounded in affection for Louise. The kids have been cheering her on throughout the book, and they continue cheering for her as she courts Serena.

It would be difficult to imagine a more blatant example of destructive indoctrination than this! The first part of the book establishes a relationship between the children and the swan so the children identify themselves with the swan. Then the teacher is encouraged to change the sex of the swan as the now-female swan courts another female swan. In this way the children find themselves in a vicarious lesbian relationship.

How many three and four year-old children are equipped to resist this kind of propaganda? None whatsoever. Obviously this NAEYC curriculum is intended to program children (social engineering), not educate them. The curriculum is intended to program our youngest and most vulnerable children with the basic building blocks of the radical new Federal Curriculum.

This kind of propaganda will have an enormous impact on our nation's children. Indeed, indoctrination programs far more timid than the one above have already had a huge impact. For example, the

Minneapolis *StarTribune* (1-28-02) reprinted a recent poll summarized by the *Los Angeles Times* as follows:

> More college freshmen today describe themselves as politically liberal than at any time since the Viet Nam War, according to a nationwide survey by researchers at the University of California, Los Angeles.
>
> A resurgence of liberalism among the freshmen is also reflected in their attitudes on a wide range of political and social issues, according to survey results released today.
>
> "It's a real change, a broad-based trend toward greater liberalism on almost every issue we look at," said Alexander Astin, an education professor at UCLA who started the survey, the nation's largest, in 1966.
>
> For instance, a record percentage—57.9 percent—think gay couples should have the right to marry....

If the new Federal Curriculum has its way, the 57.9 percent of college freshmen who support homosexual marriage will be raised to 100 percent. The ultimate goal of the new Federal Curriculum is to indoctrinate all our children to the point that all seven themes of the new Federal Curriculum are embraced by all our children—long before they are able to evaluate or in any way resist this massive propaganda program.

CHAPTER SEVENTEEN

Reconstructing History

This chapter will describe how the new Minnesota history standards (now in the process of being adopted) implement the new Federal Curriculum. The left column contains the standards, the right column contains the author's comments on these standards:

The New Standards	Author's Comments
HISTORICAL THINKING AND UNDERSTANDING	
Reflections	
True historical thinking and understanding goes far beyond a collection of stories. **History is often presented as a collection of dates, places and events and subsequently misunderstood** as being a collection of trivia rather than	Notice that the study of history has been replaced by the theme of how to think about history—as defined by the

as an intellectual discipline. Stories of famous presidents, great battles, or social movements are sometimes treated as if their value were obvious to all. History includes using historical themes to organize and analyze information. It includes the development of questioning and exploration of possibilities. **It demands that we recognize perspective and values.**

Historical themes are introduced in the primary grades. The Minnesota standard, *Family, School, and Community*, is a study of social and cultural history. It integrates the other social studies disciplines of geography, economics, and civics by **asking students to map their communities, examine wants and needs, and consider roles and responsibilities in the community.**

The central historical thinking skill - chronological thinking - is introduced at this level. Students gain a sense of past, present, and future by **examining their own history**, the history of their community, and the hopes they have for improving their community. **Even if a curriculum is literature-based,** this skill needs to be introduced and developed. Students in the primary grades also begin to use and **construct** the basic tools of the historian - the timeline and the historical narrative. At this level, students begin to see the

new standards, of course. The new standards take a negative view of teaching historical facts.

"Perspective and values" refers to the ideology of multiculturalism which replaces the teaching of genuine history. This is theme number five in the new Federal Curriculum. See Chapter 12.)

Students are taught to be political activists instead of being taught genuine history.

(All errors of grammar and punctuation, such as the use of a single hyphen for a dash instead of the required double hyphen, are recorded as written in the new Minnesota standards.)

"Examining their own history" is not studying history.

Literature is used to teach the new curriculum. Note the word "construct." (See comments below.)

116

role of **values and perspective** in the decisions people make in history and in their own decisions. They begin to understand the central historical concept of *cause and effect* because they examine how decisions and actions **in their own families** and communities had results and outcomes.

In the intermediate grades, the students' horizon's begin to expand. They begin to **incorporate the theme of science and technology** as they examine how changes have affected people over time. They expand their study of ether eras and other regions of the world. This, in turn, increases their understanding of **perspective and values** as they examine other cultures. They increase the use of historical maps and their understanding of the relationship between geography and history. They are able to **identify key people and events in history and explain why they are important.** Their timelines and historical stories become more sophisticated, showing a greater understanding of cause effect relationships, values and perspectives. They begin to develop **historical questioning skills,** asking, "Why?" and "What if? about the past. The variety and use of primary and secondary sources also should expand. Graphs, tables charts, oral histories, photos, music, art, literature are all used. Students at the intermediate level become better **at sorting facts from fiction** as they use a greater variety of sources. They also can better

The terms "values and perspectives" are used eight times in this short section. The terms are code for multiculturalism which is the real subject being taught instead of history (see Chapter 12).

Examining themselves and their families is not studying history.

The themes of the new Federal Curriculum are interdisciplinary.

This is multiculturalism, not history, and not genuine education.

These students will be at a disadvantage on anything requiring a knowledge of history, because they will have studied little genuine history.

Process is more important than knowledge, even in grades one to three.

Students can sort facts from fiction only if they have learned enough facts upon

117

articulate the ways past events have affected society today. The Minnesota standard, *Historical Events*, also introduces important concepts of conflict, cooperation and **interdependence**....

By the time Minnesota students reach the high school level, they should have a strong sense of **how to reconstruct history**. They should be comfortable with a variety of primary and secondary sources, including oral histories, quantitative data, and at least basic statistical analysis. They recognize values bias, perspective, context, and purpose in the sources they use. They can **formulate a position based on evidence**. Ideally, they can understand their own values, biases, and perspectives in the **histories that they construct** and the positions that they formulate. They can communicate through narratives, timelines, graphic organizers, oral presentations, and other media. Students can recognize themes in historical narratives and timelines. They can also use themes to organize and categorize information. Minnesota's high standards in the social studies and inquiry - *themes of United States History, Diverse Perspectives, Social Science Processes*, to name a few— are centered on these skills and understandings.

The **ultimate goal** of teaching historical thinking and understanding skills **is to develop good citizens**. If students have a strong sense of how past actions

which to base such judgments.

"Cooperation and interdependence" have replaced individual rights as the dominant value.

"Reconstructing history" is central to multiculturalism and postmodernism. That is, genuine history is replaced by the values and attitudes of the new Federal Curriculum. This is radical education.

How can students formulate a position based on evidence when the only information they learn is information selected by the multicultural worldview?

Having students construct their own histories means that historical knowledge is irrelevant. All history to them becomes subjective opinion.

"Good citizens" are defined by the new Federal Curriculum as those who have adopted the worldview of the new affect the present and our current actions could affect the future, then they may be more thoughtful about their decisions. If they understand how bias, perspective and values influence the information they receive, then they may view the media with a more critical eye. If history becomes much more than a collection of dates, names and events, then our students will actually understand its importance.

Most Key Student Understandings were adapted from the Minnesota *Social Studies* standards. Other information was taken from the following sources: **Center for Civic Education** (1994). *National standards for civics and government.* Calabasas CA: Author.... [Emphasis added.]

education system and have become political activists in support of it.

What about the bias involved in replacing history with multiculturalism?

That is, Minnesota's new history standards are in conformity with the *National Standards for Civics and Government* written by the CCE.

It is apparent from the history standards recorded above that the real theme being taught is that of "constructing" or "reconstructing" history. This focal point of the standards, as stated by Minnesota's new history standards, is the following:

> By the time Minnesota students reach the high school level, they should have a strong sense of how to **reconstruct history**. [Emphasis added.]

And, again:

> Ideally, they [high school students] can understand their own values, biases, and perspectives in the **histories they construct** and the positions they formulate. [Emphasis added.]

In education circles, "constructing history" has a clearly defined meaning. That meaning was identified in an article appearing in the

Minneapolis *Star Tribune*, 2-19-98, written by University of Minnesota Law School Professors, Suzanna Sherry and Daniel Farber, who said:

> American constitutional democracy is a product of the idea that we can all aspire to objective truth and justice. Nothing is true because the president, the pope, or the *New York Times* says it is. Knowledge is accessible to all who seek it.
>
> But over the past decade, some radical law professors have been...claiming that there is no such thing as truth or knowledge or merit or reason. All these things...are simply a mask for racism, sexism and other pathologies.
>
> According to the radicals...there is no truth, just individual **perspectives** based on race, gender and the like—and everyone's **perspective** is equally valid. Indeed, they argue, there is no such thing as objective reality. Reality is **"socially constructed"** by the powerful....[Emphasis added.]

This is the radical philosophy known as "postmodernism" (there is no genuine truth or morality.) What we believe is true or morally right are merely ideas [constructs] formulated by the powerful to keep the vulnerable under subjection. (Postmodernist ideology is central to multiculturalism, also called "diversity" and "tolerance.")

The idea is this: What we have traditionally thought was history, including our views of men like George Washington, Thomas Jefferson, and Abraham Lincoln, is not real history, or real truth at all. Our views of such people are mere "constructs." That is, our views were formulated by rich and powerful white males for the purpose of keeping the rest of the population under their control. According to the postmodernists, all supposed history consists of constructs—propaganda used by the powerful for subjugating the weak and vulnerable (the central tenet of Marxism).

The solution to this exploitation of the poor by the rich, says the postmodernist, is to first "deconstruct" history (remove the supposed historical facts of the past), and then to "reconstruct" history (rewrite history in order to reveal that it was really all about the rich white males exploiting everybody else), and then to create our own "constructs" (revealing that all classes, nationalities, moral systems, religions, forms of government, etc. are equal and that the powerful groups have systematically exploited vulnerable people and classes.) This radical view of history is now the required unifying theme of the new history standards that all our students must be taught and tested on. (Non-public students will be at an extreme disadvantage on any of the "achievement" tests if they have not been indoctrinated in this postmodernist view of history.)

Does this mean that students will now be allowed to decide for themselves what the real history, if any, actually is? Not at all. The only history that students will learn are those items which appear to be consistent with the views of the new Federal Curriculum. The new system is all about indoctrination, not education. The federal government, through its agent the Center for Civic Education, has determined what is true, valuable and right. Federally defined knowledge, attitudes, and values are the only ones that will be tolerated. Anyone who subscribes to a different worldview will be marginalized and relegated to the back seat on the bus.

As Richard Bernstein correctly said, "Multiculturalism is a code word for a left-wing political program." This left-wing (and radical) political program now forms a key element of the new core curriculum in America's new education system. The irony of it all is that the architects of the new history standards actually make history into the propaganda tool that they claim (falsely) it has always been in traditional (and academic) education. The designers of the new system accuse others of what they are doing themselves.

CHAPTER EIGHTEEN

Requiring the NAEP Test

The NAEP test is the federal government's primary enforcement mechanism for the new Federal Curriculum. "NAEP" is an acronym for National Assessment of Educational Progress. The NAEP is also called "the nation's report card."

The NAEP is the one and only "achievement" test administered by the federal government. The last federal education funding bill, HR1, passed in 2002, stipulates that all fifty states must now administer the NAEP test by force of federal law. That law allows the U.S. Department of Education to determine how completely each state is implementing the new Federal Curriculum.

Keep in mind, that the test always drives the curriculum. The content of the NAEP test determines the content of the curriculum each state must now teach its students. In addition, the other common national achievement tests, as well as the state tests, are following the lead of the NAEP. For example, on May 23, 2002, the *New York Times* reported that the College Board is totally redesigning the SAT test. The *Times* said:

...his [the Board Chairman's] description of the goals of the process **reflect a profound change,** turning what was **once specifically deemed an aptitude, or intelligence test**—until 1990, the SAT stood for Scholastic Aptitude Test—into an achievement test **designed to measure what is learned in the classroom.** [Emphasis added.]

In other words, the SAT used to measure the student's ability and likelihood to succeed in college. Not any more. Now the SAT will measure what the student has been taught in school–as defined by the new Federal Curriculum.

Table 8 below describes the themes included, and not included, in the language arts section of the 11th grade NAEP test. (The 11th grade NAEP is the highest level NAEP test.) Those themes, as revealed by the categories of key terms, and their frequency of use, are as follows:

Table 8
Number of Times Key Terms Are Used in the NAEP

Terms relating to environmentalism 14
Terms relating to multiculturalism. 18
Terms relating to vocationalism 39
Terms relating to any aspect of geography. 0
Terms relating to any aspect of history,
other than Native American history 0
Terms relating to any aspect of American
Government, including national sovereignty,
natural law, or any of the natural rights 0

Table 9 below identifies the particular terms used in the different categories, along with the frequency of their use:

Table 9
Number of Times Specific Terms Are Used in the NAEP

Terms relating to environmentalism
"Spider's web". 1
"Mother Earth" (capital letters), ... 2

Terms relating to multiculturalism

Terms relating to vocationalism

As can be seen from the two tables above, the language arts portion of the NAEP test includes numerous questions dealing with themes of environmentalism, multiculturalism, and vocationalism. The traditional academic subjects, however, such as history, geography, and American government, have been largely excluded—the reason being that the NAEP has been designed to impose the new Federal Curriculum on all fifty states.

The NAEP even includes a writing test question which requires students to write a letter to elected officials advising the officials to spend tax dollars on certain projects. In this way, the NAEP requires all students who take the test to become political activists (see Chapters 2 ,16 & 17). At the same time, the NAEP is constructed to enable the measurement of the percentage of students in each state, year by year, who are committed to the radical political agenda of the new Federal Curriculum.

As we have seen previously, this new Federal Curriculum is not an academic curriculum; it is a curriculum of attitudes, values and belief. That is, it's a curriculum intended to teach a clearly defined worldview, a worldview which forms the philosophical and religious basis for a one-world government.

Why, then, don't parents and lawmakers object to the content of the NAEP? How can they object when they don't know what is on the test? The federal law which requires all states to administer the NAEP (HR1) also makes it a felony to disclose any of the NAEP questions. (Title VI, Sec. 411, c. 4.) That is why this book summarizes what those questions cover but avoids mentioning any question word for word, even though this author has a copy of the NAEP.

This shroud of secrecy over the NAEP questions is a clear violation of the United States Constitution. The First Amendment to the Constitution states: "*Congress shall make no law...abridging the freedom of speech....*"

It is recognized that there are two exceptions to this law, those exceptions being national security and the safety of all U.S. citizens. The NAEP test, however, has nothing to do with national security, nor does its secrecy have any bearing on the safety of our citizens. The content of the NAEP is so outrageous that a shroud of secrecy, enforced by federal law, must be in place to prevent the test from being discredited. (It is actually the radical agenda of the NAEP, protected by federal law, which is a genuine threat to our national security and to the safety of all our citizens.) The new Federal Curriculum intends to rewrite the Constitution, not follow it.

At the same time, federal bureaucrats have their ways of letting the state bureaucrats know what is on the NAEP so the state curricula and guidelines can be written accordingly.

CHAPTER NINETEEN

Requiring the New Federal Curriculum

This chapter will describe how one state (Minnesota) has adopted the new Federal Curriculum and is requiring all its public schools to adopt the curriculum, as well. The new curriculum is described in *A Guide for Curriculum Development to Support Minnesota's High Standards*, published by the State of Minnesota in early 2002 (no publication date is given).

This Minnesota *Guide for Curriculum* consists of eight booklets, one for each "learning area." Each booklet begins with the same introduction, which says:

> This guide outlines the **key concepts and skills that students must acquire** to achieve Minnesota's High Standards.... In addition, **educators must ensure** that **all specifications of a content standard are embedded** in their locally developed and adopted curriculum. [Emphasis added, p. 1 of each booklet.]

As can be seen from the above quotation, this new curriculum must be taught by all public schools and all public school teachers. There is nothing optional about it. The term "locally developed and adopted curriculum" is typical of the propaganda in the new Federal Curriculum. "Locally developed" is meaningless when the state tells the schools and the teachers what they must teach.

What is this curriculum that all public schools and teachers in Minnesota now must teach? The overview of the *Guide for Curriculum* for literature and nonfiction says the following:

> Reading, viewing and listening to good literature **connects us to one another and broadens our worldview**.... High School students understand how literature and other artistic works help them develop a more **tolerant worldview** and a greater acceptance of others' lives, points of view, and histories. [p.2] Students need to be able to access the records of many cultures of our world to help them understand and accept who they are as individuals, as well as within the **collective society**, and to **grow in tolerance** and awareness in an ever more **global society**. [Emphasis added, p. 7.]

Students must adopt a "tolerant worldview" within a "collective society" which leads us to a "global society." That is, the real curriculum in the *Read Listen and View* portion of Minnesota's required curriculum is the radical worldview of multiculturalism culminating in one-world government. (See Chapters 12 and 13 of this book.) As we have seen, multiculturalism and one-world government are two of the themes required by the new Federal Curriculum.

In the *Social Studies* portion of Minnesota's new required curriculum, we find that the first portion of this curriculum is called **"Citizenship and Community."** What might the word "community" mean in this context? The *Guide for Curriculum* explains:

> Throughout this system of K-12 citizenship and community education, students are guided to a deeper understanding of what it means to be a citizen of the United

States with inherent rights and responsibilities as individuals and as **members of the larger community.** [Emphasis added, p. 2.]

What community is larger than the United States? The world community, of course. This notion of "world citizenship" is developed throughout this *Guide for Curriculum.* The *Guide,* for example, also states:

At this level, the curriculum addresses the importance of government as a vehicle to promote rules and laws **designed to protect the common good and individual rights.** [Emphasis added, p. 2.]

Is that the role of government? To "protect the common good" (as defined by government) and individual rights equally? As we saw in Chapter 9 of this book, the U.S. Declaration of Independence states that government has one fundamental goal, not two. That goal is stated by the Declaration as follows: *"That, to secure these rights, Governments are instituted among Men...."*

The Declaration of Independence states plainly that government has one primary purpose, not two. The Declaration clarifies that this one fundamental purpose of government is protecting the individual rights, especially the rights of life, liberty and property. In our nation's foundational documents, the so-called "common good" is never put on the same level as protecting the basic human rights.

Where, then, did this theme of "protecting the common good and individual rights" come from? The *National Standards for Civics and Government* states:

Explain that the purposes of government in the United Stated are to protect the rights of individuals and to promote the common good. [P. 17.]

As is evident from the above quotations, Minnesota's new *Guide for Curriculum* takes its view of human rights from the new Federal Curriculum, not from our nation's authoritative documents. As we saw in Chapter 9 of this book, the Federal Curriculum's definition of human rights is the internationalist (and communist) definition, not the definition that formed the basis for freedom in the United States of America.

As the *National Standards for Civics and Government* correctly said:

> They [the founders of the United States] argued that the **principle purpose of government is the protection of individual rights, the "unalienable rights to life, liberty and the pursuit of happiness,"** of which Jefferson spoke inthe Declaration of Independence. [Emphasis added, p. 8.]

It is this understanding (that protection of the natural rights is the principle purpose of government) that is undermined in the new Federal Curriculum and in Minnesota's new required curriculum. This foundational principle of freedom—that government exists to protect the basic human rights—is eliminated by the new Federal Curriculum and Minnesota's curriculum and is replaced by the internationalist view that government has two basic purposes. This internationalist view of human rights is embodied in the Universal Declaration of Human Rights, 1948. (See Chapter 15 and the Appendixes.)

What else is required by the new Minnesota curriculum? Following are some additional requirements:

> They also need to compare ways "that people from different cultures deal with the physical environment. [P. 7 of *Social Studies*, see Chapter 11 of this book on environmentalism.]
> By the time Minnesota students reach the high school level, they should have a strong sense of how to **construct history**. [P. 18 of *Social Studies*, see Chapter 12 of this book on multiculturalism.]
> Data investigation can be a powerful means of connecting mathematics to the lives of children, to news events, and to other disciplines in the curriculum. [P. 2 of *Mathematical Concepts and Applications*, meaning that the new Federal Curriculum must also be taught in math classes, see Chapter 3.]

At the **Primary** level, students will: increase awareness of and observe a variety of traditional and non-traditional careers [and] become aware of decision making skills as they relate to exploring and understanding career opportunities in a changing world. [P. 5 of *Career Investigation*. In Minnesota, education is now nothing more than career training starting in pre-school and kindergarten.]

In summary, this is how the new Minnesota required curriculum teaches all the themes of the new Federal Curriculum:

Theme 1: Undermining National Sovereignty. (The new Minnesota *Guide for Curriculum Development* never mentions national sovereignty. Out of sight is out of mind.)

Theme 2: Redefining Natural Rights. (The new Minnesota *Guide for Curriculum Development* replaces the actual and historical view of human rights with the internationalist/Marxist view.)

Theme 3: Minimizing Natural Law. (The new Minnesota *Guide for Curriculum Development* never mentions natural law. Once again, out of sight is out of mind.)

Theme 4: Promoting Environmentalism. (The new Minnesota *Guide for Curriculum Development* requires that environmentalism be taught under the *Social Studies* framework.)

Theme 5: Requiring Multiculturalism. (The new Minnesota *Guide for Curriculum Development* redefines history so that history becomes multiculturalism. Language arts are also reconstructed to require multiculturalism.)

Theme 6: Restructuring Government. (The new Minnesota *Guide for Curriculum Development*, *Social Studies* section, redefines "citizenship" to mean "world citizenship," "community" to mean "world community," and "society" to mean "global society.")

Theme 7: Redefining Education as Job Skills. (The new Minnesota *Guide for Curriculum Development, Career Development* section, clarifies that all education now exists for the purpose of career training.)

As is evident, Minnesota's new required curriculum is a perfect match to the new Federal Curriculum. This, of course, is the plan—the curriculum of each state must match the new Federal Curriculum. The federal government will use the NAEP test to make sure that this is actually happening in every state.

The new Federal Curriculum is not limited to just the curriculum taught in every school, of course. The *National Standards for Civics Education* stipulates that the Federal Curriculum must form the basis for all of the following (underlining added):

A. **Teachers.** Content Standards provide teachers with clear statements of <u>what they should teach their students</u>.

B. **Teacher education and credentialing institutions.** Standards provide teacher education and credentialing institutions with <u>clear guidelines for training teachers and granting credentials</u>.

C. **Assessment specialists.** Standards are <u>essential</u> to the development of assessment programs designed to determine acceptable levels of performance.

D. **Parents and community.** Standards will provide parents and other community members with understandable information about <u>what should be taught and learned in K-12 education</u>.

E. **Curriculum developers.** Standards provide guidance for the development of high quality curricular programs, <u>textbooks, and other related educational materials</u>.

F. **Policy makers.** Standards and evidence of their achievement provide a rational basis for the development and implementation of public policy in education.

As can be seen from the above quotation, the new Federal Curriculum exists to take control over every aspect of education in America.

PART IV

The Road Back

Chapter Twenty

Restoring America

As we have seen, the education system of our nation has been taken over by those who wish to restructure all of America. Education in our nation used to be dedicated to the pursuit of knowledge, truth and virtue. Education is now dedicated to indoctrinating our children with clearly defined attitudes, values and behaviors—a comprehensive worldview—a worldview that is hostile to freedom and that culminates in the dismemberment of our nation's fundamental principles and the elimination of our national sovereignty. The ultimate goal of the new curriculum is the establishment of a one-world government which will mean the end of all our basic rights, including life, liberty and property, and will reduce us all to being serfs of an elitist, totalitarian world-state.

The architects of this utopian dream intend to be the individuals who will rule the world. Theirs is the dream of Alexander the Great, Adolph Hitler and Joseph Stalin all rolled into one.

This new education system can only exist under the cover of misrepresentation, distortion and outright lies. The American public and its legislators would have no sympathy for this new system, if they only knew what it was. Lawmakers, for example, are told that they are establishing a curriculum that will "teach our children the Bill of Rights." These same lawmakers have no idea that the new system actually undermines our Bill of Rights and substitutes in its place the internationalist/Marxist view of human rights—which means that there are no human rights whatsoever.

Behind this deception of the radicals, however, lies the answer to the restoration of America. If American citizens find out what the new education system really is, the public will demand that it be thrown out and that American education be restored to being a knowledge-based system. Informing the public is the key. Informing the public is the only means by which our nation can be restored. Informing the public is the only way our great republic can be saved.

Today is not too late. Tomorrow may be. If the new Federal Curriculum is not thrown out, our generation will be the last generation in America to understand what genuine freedom means. Our generation will be the last generation to understand what the foundational principles of our nation actually are.

Every generation in our nation has had to fight the battle for freedom in some way. The attack now being waged against our country by the new Federal Curriculum is the primary battle for freedom in our time. To lose this battle is to lose everything our nation has ever fought for. To lose this battle is to lose everything that millions of brave Americans have ever risked their lives, and have given their lives, to preserve.

Truth always precedes freedom. America will remain free only if its citizens know what is true. Those of us who understand what is happening must bring this truth to those who do not know.

The media, for the most part, will not help us. The media now exists to support the new system, not to report on it. Walter Cronkite, for example, was totally committed to one-world government. There are others in the media who share that commitment.

What if ten percent of the public knew what was happening and were committed to rescuing our nation? Would that be enough to turn around this attack against our nation? It would be more than enough. It takes less than ten percent to decide most elections. Most lawmakers will do whatever a committed ten percent wants them to do, especially when the other 90 percent doesn't know and/or doesn't care.

This means that the preservation of our nation is up to you, the reader. This author is only one person. The publisher of this book, Maple River Education Coalition (MrEdCo), is only one organization. We try to do our part, but the success of our effort depends upon you. *You* hold the key to whether our nation survives or is destroyed.

Sir Winston Churchill commended the Royal Air Force of Britain by saying: "Never before in the field of human conflict was so much owed by so many to so few." These same words may also apply to you, the reader. Our future is in your hands. Our nation depends upon you. Our nation needs your total commitment. Tell your friends. Give or loan them copies of this book. Give or loan them copies of the video which summarizes this book.

Our nation has always depended on the commitment of its citizens to keep it free. Such is surely the case today. It has never been more true than today. Truth always precedes freedom, and there is no freedom without the truth. May God grant that you, the reader, do your part in distributing the truth that alone can keep our nation free.

Allen Quist

Appendix A

The Declaration of Independence

In Congress, July 4, 1776

The Unanimous Declaration of the Thirteen United States of America

When in the Course of human events it becomes necessary for one people to dissolve the political bands which have connected them with another, and to assume, among the Powers of the earth, the separate and equal station to which the Laws of Nature and of Nature's God entitle them, a decent respect to the opinions of mankind requires that they should declare the causes which impel them to the separation.

We hold these truths to be self-evident, that all men are created equal, that they are endowed by their Creator with certain unalienable Rights, that among these are Life, Liberty and the pursuit of Happiness. That to secure these rights, Governments are instituted among Men, deriving their just powers from the consent of the governed. That whenever any Form of Government becomes destructive of these ends, it is the Right of the People to alter or to abolish it, and to institute new Government, laying its foundation on such principles and organizing its powers in such form, as to them shall seem most likely to effect their Safety and Happiness. Prudence, indeed, will dictate that Governments long established should not be changed for light and transient causes; and accordingly all experience hath shewn that mankind are more disposed to suffer, while evils are sufferable, than to right themselves by abolishing the forms to which they are accustomed. But when a long train of abuses and usurpations, pursuing invariably the same Object evinces a design to reduce them under absolute Despotism, it is their right, it is their duty, to throw off such Government, and to provide new Guards for their future security. Such has been the patient sufferance of these Colonies; and such is now the necessity which constrains them to alter their former Systems of Government. The history of the present King of Great Britain is a history of repeated injuries and usurpations, all having in direct object the establishment of an absolute Tyranny over these States. To prove this, let Facts be submitted to a candid world.

He has refused his Assent to Laws, the most wholesome and necessary for the public good.

He has forbidden his Governors to pass Laws of immediate and pressing importance, unless suspended in their operation till his Assent should be obtained; and when so suspended, he has utterly neglected to attend to them.

He has refused to pass other Laws for the accommodations of large districts of people, unless those people would relinquish the right of Representation in the Legislature, a right inestimable to them and formidable to tyrants only.

He has called together legislative bodies at places unusual, uncomfortable, and distant from the depository of their Public Records, for the sole purpose of fatiguing them into compliance with his measures.

He has dissolved Representative Houses repeatedly, for opposing with manly firmness his invasions on the rights of the people.

He has refused for a long time, after such dissolutions, to cause others to be elected; whereby the Legislative Powers, incapable of Annihilation, have returned to the People at large for their exercise; the State remaining in the mean time exposed to all the dangers of invasion from without, and convulsions within.

He has endeavored to prevent the population of these States; for that purpose obstructing the Laws of Naturalization of Foreigners; refusing to pass others to encourage their migration hither, and raising the conditions of new Appropriations of Lands.

He has obstructed the Administration of Justice, by refusing his Assent to Laws for establishing Judiciary Powers.

He has made Judges dependent on his Will alone, for the tenure of their offices, and the amount and payment of their salaries.

He has erected a multitude of New Offices, and sent hither swarms of Officers to harass our People, and eat out of their substance.

He has kept among us, in times of peace, Standing Armies without the Consent of our legislatures.

He has affected to render the Military independent of and superior to the Civil power.

He has combined with others to subject us to a jurisdiction foreign to our constitution, and unacknowledged by our laws; giving his Assent to their Acts of pretended Legislations.

For quartering large bodies of armed troops among us:

For protecting them, by a mock Trial, from punishment for any Murders which they should commit on the Inhabitants of these States:

For cutting off our Trade with all parts of the world:

For imposing taxes on us without our Consent:

For depriving us in many cases, of the benefits of Trial by Jury:

For transporting us beyond Seas to be tried for pretended offences:

For abolishing the free System of English Laws in a neighboring Province, establishing therein an Arbitrary government, and enlarging its Boundaries so as to render it at once an example and fit instrument for introducing the same absolute rule into these Colonies:

For taking away our Charters, abolishing our most valuable Laws, and altering fundamentally the Forms of our Governments:

For suspending our own Legislatures and declaring themselves invested with Power to legislate for us in all cases whatsoever.

He has abdicated Government here, by declaring us out of his Protection and waging War against us.

He has plundered our seas, ravaged our Coasts, burnt our towns, and destroyed the lives of our people.

He is at this time transporting large Armies of foreign Mercenaries to compleat the works of death, desolation and tyranny, already begun with circumstances of Cruelty and perfidy scarcely paralleled in the most barbarous ages, and totally unworthy the Head of a civilized nation.

He has constrained our fellow Citizens taken Captive on the high Seas to bear Arms against their Country, to become the executioners of their friends and Brethren, or to fall themselves by their Hands.

He has excited domestic insurrections amongst us, and has endeavored to bring on the inhabitants of our frontiers, the merciless Indian Savages, whose known rule of warfare, is an undistinguished destruction of all ages, sexes and conditions.

In every stage of these Oppressions We have Petitioned for Redress in the most humble terms: Our repeated Petitions have been answered only by repeated injury: A Prince, whose character is thus marked by every act which may define a Tyrant, is unfit to be the ruler of a free people.

Nor have We been wanting in attention to our British brethren. We have warned them from time to time of attempts by their legislature to extend an unwarrantable jurisdiction over us. We have reminded them of the circumstances of our emigration and settlement here. We have appealed to their native justice and magnanimity; and we have conjured them by the ties of our common kindred to disavow these usurpations, which would inevitably interrupt our connections and correspondence. They too have been deaf to the voice of justice and consanguinity. We must, therefore, acquiesce in the necessity, which denounces our Separation, and hold them, as we hold the rest of mankind, Enemies in War, in Peace Friends.

We, therefore, the Representatives of the United States of America, in General Congress, Assembled, appealing to the Supreme Judge of the world for the rectitude of our intentions, do in the Name, and by the Authority of the good People of these Colonies, solemnly publish and declare, That these United States are, and of Right ought to be Free and Independent States; that they are Absolved from all Allegiance to the British Crown, and that all political connection between them and the State of Great Britain is, and ought to be totally dissolved; and that as Free and Independent States, they have full Power to levy War, conclude Peace, contract Alliances, establish Commerce, and to do all other Acts and Things which Independent States may of right do. And for the support of this Declaration, with a firm reliance on the Protection of divine Providence, we mutually pledge to each other our Lives, our Fortunes and our sacred Honor.

Georgia:
Button Gwinnett
Lyman Hall
George Walton

North Carolina:
William Hooper
Joseph Hewes
John Penn

South Carolina:
Edward Rutledge
Thomas Heyward, Jr.
Thomas Lynch, Jr.
Arthur Middleton

Massachusetts:
John Hancock

Maryland:
Samuel Chase
William Paca
Thomas Stone
Charles Carroll of
  Carrollton

Virginia:
George Wythe
Richard Henry Lee

Thomas Jefferson
Benjamin Harrison
Thomas Nelson, Jr.
Francis Lightfoot Lee
Carter Braxton

Pennsylvania:
Robert Morris
Benjamin Rush
Benjamin Franklin
John Morton
George Clymer
James Smith
George Taylor
James Wilson
George Ross

Delaware:
Caesar Rodney
George Read
Thomas McKean

New York:
William Floyd
Philip Livingston
Francis Lewis
Lewis Morris

New Jersey:
Richard Stockton
John Witherspoon
Francis Hopkinson
John Hart
Abraham Clark

New Hampshire:
Josiah Bartlett
William Whipple

Massachusetts:
Samuel Adams
John Adams
Robert Treat Paine
Elbridge Gerry

Rhode Island:
Stephen Hopkins
William Ellery

Connecticut:
Roger Sherman
Samuel Huntington
William Williams
Oliver Wolcott

New Hampshire:
Matthew Thornton

Universal Declaration of Human Rights [1948]

PREAMBLE

Whereas recognition of the inherent dignity and of the equal and inalienable rights of all members of the human family is the foundation of freedom, justice and peace in the world,

Whereas disregard and contempt for human rights have resulted in barbarous acts which have outraged the conscience of mankind, and the advent of a world in which human beings shall enjoy freedom of speech and belief and freedom from fear and want has been proclaimed as the highest aspiration of the common people,

Whereas it is essential, if man is not to be compelled to have recourse, as a last resort, to rebellion against tyranny and oppression, the human rights should be protected by the rule of law,

Whereas it is essential to promote the development of friendly relations between nations,

Whereas the peoples of the United Nations have in the Charter reaffirmed their faith in fundamental human rights, in the dignity and worth of the human person and in the equal rights of men and women and have determined to promote social progress and better standards of life in larger freedom,

Whereas Member States have pledged themselves to achieve, in co-operation with the United Nations, the promotion of universal respect for and observance of human rights and fundamental freedoms,

Whereas a common understanding of these rights and freedoms is of the greatest importance for the full realization of this pledge,

Now, therefore,

The General Assembly

Proclaims this Universal Declaration of Human Rights as a common standard of achievement for all peoples and all nations to the end that every individual and every organization of society, keeping this Declaration constantly in mind, shall strive by teaching and education to promote the respect for these rights and freedoms and by progressive measures, national and international, to secure their universal and effective recognition and observance, both among the peoples of Member States themselves and among the peoples of territories under their jurisdiction.

Article 1

All human beings are born free and equal in dignity and rights. They are endowed with reason and conscience and should act towards one another in a spirit of brotherhood.

Article 2

Everyone is entitled to all the rites and freedoms set forth in this Declaration, without distinction of any kind, such as race, color, sex language, religion, political or other opinion, national or social origin, property, birth or other status.

Furthermore, no distinction shall be made on the basis of the political, jurisdictional or international status of the country or territory to which a person belongs, whether it be independent, trust, non-self-governing or under any other limitation of sovereignty.

Article 3

Everyone has the right of life, liberty and the security of person.

Article 4

No one shall be held in slavery or servitude; slavery and the slave trade shall be prohibited in all their forms.

Article 5

No one shall be subjected to torture or to cruel, inhuman or degrading treatment of punishment.

Article 6

Everyone has the right to recognition everywhere as a person before the law.

Article 7

All are equal before the law and are entitled without an discrimination to equal protection of the law. All are entitled to equal protection against any discrimination in violation of this Declaration and against any incitement to such discrimination.

Article 8

Everyone has the right to an effective remedy by the competent national tribunals for acts violating the fundamental rights against him by the constitution or by law.

Article 9

No one shall be subjected to arbitrary arrest, detention or exile

Article 10

Everyone is entitled in full equality to a fair, and public hearing by an independent and impartial tribunal in the determination of his rights and obligations and of any criminal charge against him.

Article 11

1. Everyone charged with a penal offence has the right to be presumed innocent until proved guilty according to law in a public trail at which he has had all the guarantees necessary for his defence.

2. No one shall be held guilty of any penal offence on account of any act or omission which did not constitute a penal offence, under national or international law, at the time when it was committed. Nor shall a heavier penalty be imposed than the one that was applicable at the time the penal offence was committed.

Article 12

No one shall be subjected to arbitrary interference with his privacy, family, home or correspondence, nor to attacks upon his honour and reputation. Everyone has the right to the protection of the law against such interference or attacks.

Article 13

1. Everyone has the right to freedom of movement and residence within the borders of each State.

2. Everyone has the right to leave any country, including his own, and to return to his country.

Article 14

1. Everyone has the right to seek and to enjoy in other countries asylum from persecution.

2. This right may not be invoked in the case of prosecutions genuinely arising from non-political crimes or from acts contrary to the purposes and principles of the United Nations.

Article 15

1. Everyone has the right to a nationality.

2. No one shall be arbitrarily deprived of his nationality nor denied the right to change his nationality.

Article 16

1. Men and women of full age, without any limitation due to race nationality or religion, have the right to marry and to found a family. They are entitled to equal rights as to marriage, during marriage and at its dissolution.

2. Marriage shall be entered into only with the free and full consent of the intending spouses.

3. The family is the natural and fundamental group unit of society and is entitled to protection by society and the State.

Article 17

1. Everyone has the right to own property alone as well as in association with others.

2. No one shall be arbitrarily deprived of his property.

Article 18

Everyone has the right to freedom of thought, conscience and religion; this right includes freedom to change his religion or belief, and freedom, either alone or in community with others and in public or private, to manifest his religion or belief in teaching, practice, worship and observance.

Article 19

Everyone has the right to freedom of opinion and expression; this right includes freedom to hold opinions without interference and to seek, receive and impart information and ideas through any media and regardless of frontiers.

Article 20

1. Everyone has the right to freedom of peaceful assembly and association.

2. No one may be compelled to belong to an association.

Article 21

1. Everyone has the right to take part in the government of his country, directly or through freely chosen representatives.

2. Everyone has the right of equal access to public service in his country.

3. The will of the people shall be the basis of the authority of government; this will shall be expressed in periodic and genuine elections which shall be by universal and equal suffrage and shall be held by secret vote or by equivalent free voting procedures.

Article 22

Everyone, as a member of society, has the right to social security and is entitled to realization, through national effort and international co-operation and in accordance with the organization and resources of each State, of the economic, social and cultural rights indispensable for his dignity and the free development of his personality.

Article 23

1. Everyone has the right to work, to free choice of employment, to just and favourable conditions of work and to protection against unemployment.

2. Everyone, without any discrimination, has the right to equal pay for equal work.

3. Everyone who works has the right to just and favourable remuneration ensuring for himself and his family an existence worthy of human dignity, and supplemented, if necessary, by other means of social protection.

4. Everyone has the right to form and to join trade unions for the protection of his interests.

Article 24

Everyone has the right to rest and leisure, including reasonable limitation of working hours and periodic holidays with pay.

Article 25

1. Everyone has the right to a standard of living adequate for the health and well-being of himself and of his family, including food, clothing, housing and medical care and necessary social services, and the right to security in the event of unemployment, sickness, disability, widowhood, old age or other lack of livelihood in circumstances beyond his control.

2. Motherhood and childhood are entitled to special care and assistance. All children, whether from in or out of wedlock, shall enjoy the same social protection.

Article 26

1. Everyone has the right to education. Education shall be free, at least in the elementary and fundamental stages. Elementary education shall be compulsory. Technical and professional education shall be made generally available and higher education shall be equally accessible to all on the basis of merit.

2. Education shall be directed to the full development of the human personality and to the strengthening of respect for human rights and fundamental mental freedoms. It shall promote understanding, tolerance and friendship among all nations, racial or religious groups, and shall further the activities of the United Nations for the maintenance of peace.

3. Parents have a prior right to choose the kind of education that shall be given to their children.

Article 27

1. Everyone has the right freely to participate in the cultural life of the community, to enjoy the arts and to share in scientific advancement and its benefits.

2. Everyone has the right to the protection of the moral and material interests resulting from any scientific, literary or artistic production of which he is the author.

Article 28

Everyone is entitled to a social and international order in which the rights and freedoms set forth in this Declaration can be fully realized.

Article 29

1. Everyone has duties to the community in which alone the free and full development of his personality is possible.

2. In the exercise of his rights and freedoms, everyone shall be subject only to such limitations as are determined by law solely for the purpose of securing due recognition and respect for the rights and freedoms of others and of meeting the just requirements of morality, public order and the general welfare in a democratic society.

3. These rights and freedoms may in no case be exercised contrary to the purposes and principles of the United Nations.

Article 30

Nothing in this Declaration may be interpreted as implying for any State, group or person any right to engage in any activity or to perform any act aimed at the destruction of any of the rights and freedoms set forth herein.

ABOUT THE AUTHOR

Allen Quist is the author of three other books, the most recent being *The Seamless Web: Minnesota's New Education System*, published by Maple River Education Coalition.

Mr. Quist served three terms in the Minnesota House of Representatives from 1983 to 1988. In the Minnesota House, he served as Chair of the Social Services Subcommittee and also served on the House Education Committee. He was chief author of numerous bills including the bill that created Minnesota's Department of Jobs and Training. Mr. Quist played an influential role in legalizing home schools in Minnesota. He was the Republican endorsed candidate for Governor in 1994, and was one of seven delegates elected from Minnesota to the White House Conference on Families in 1980.

Allen Quist has been a member of two school boards and holds a Bachelor of Arts Degree from Gustavus Adolphus College, a Master of Arts degree from Mankato State University, and a Bachelor of Divinity degree from Bethany Lutheran Theological Seminary. He is currently Professor of Political Science at Bethany Lutheran College in Mankato, Minnesota. Mr. Quist is a widely recognized writer and speaker in Minnesota and throughout the United States. He, his wife Julie, and the youngest three of their ten children live in rural St. Peter, Minnesota.